D0382654

100
muffins
from 1 easy recipe

100 muffins

from 1 easy recipe

This edition published in 2011

LOVE FOOD is an imprint of Parragon Books Ltd

Parragon
Queen Street House
4 Queen Street
Bath BA1 1HE, UK

Copyright © Parragon Books Ltd 2008

LOVE FOOD and the accompanying heart device is a registered trade mark
of Parragon Books Ltd in Australia, the UK, USA, India, and the EU.

www.parragon.com

All rights reserved. No part of this publication may be reproduced, stored
in a retrieval system, or transmitted, in any form or by any means,
electronic, mechanical, photocopying, recording, or otherwise, without
the prior permission of the copyright holder.

ISBN: 978-1-4454-6259-2

Printed in China

Cover design by Talking Design
Written by Susanna Tee
Internal design by Simon Levy
Photography by Clive Bozzard-Hill
Food styling by Sandra Baddeley, Carol Tennant, and Philippa Vanstone

Notes for the Reader
This book uses standard kitchen measuring spoons and cups. All spoon
and cup measurements are level unless otherwise indicated. Unless
otherwise stated, milk is assumed to be whole, eggs are large, individual
vegetables are medium, and pepper is freshly ground black pepper.

The times given are only an approximate guide. Preparation times differ
according to the techniques used by different people and the cooking
times may also vary from those given. Optional ingredients, variations,
or serving suggestions have not been included in the calculations.

Recipes using raw or very lightly cooked eggs should be avoided by
infants, the elderly, pregnant women, convalescents, and anyone with a
chronic illness. Pregnant and breast-feeding women are advised to avoid
eating peanuts and peanut products. People with nut allergies should be
aware that some of the prepared ingredients used in the recipes in this
book may contain nuts. Always check the packaging before use.

Contents

Introduction

A freshly baked muffin, sitting in its paper liner, looks so tempting and is an individual treat for both children and adults! Nothing is holding you back from making a batch because most are quick and easy to make and you probably already have most of the ingredients in your pantry. The beauty of this book is that every single recipe is based on the Basic Muffin Mix (page 10). To make life easier for you, we have done the hard work so that each recipe is complete and you won't need to refer back to the basic recipe every time.

Equipment

A large bowl, pitcher, sifter, spoon, set of measuring cups and spoons, muffin pan, and wire rack are really all you need to make most muffins.

Choose a muffin pan that has rounded corners and seamless cups. Nonstick muffin pans are available, as are silicone muffin molds. The standard-size muffin pan has 6 or 12 cup-shaped depressions, while jumbo-size muffin pans have 6 depressions and mini-size ones usually have 12 or 24 depressions. Savory muffins are particularly good baked in a mini muffin pan, especially if you want to serve them at a cocktail party. You can use the recipes in this book to make 48 mini muffins instead of the 12 standard muffins; they can be cooked for about 15 minutes.

Muffin paper liners, available in several sizes, can be placed inside the depressions in the muffin pan and will prevent any difficulties in getting the muffins out of the pan. Paper liners also help to keep the muffin moist and make transporting them for a picnic or in a lunch box easy, but they are not essential as the muffins can be baked directly in the muffin pan. However, if you do this, it is important to grease the pan with oil or melted butter for easy removal. It is best to bake savory muffins directly in the pan so that they have a crust.

The Basic Ingredients

All-purpose flour combined with baking powder gives the best rise and when an acid ingredient, such as yogurt, is used, baking soda (an alkali) is usually necessary to balance the acid/alkali proportion. Other flours and grains can be substituted for part of the flour. Use up to half the quantity of an alternative flour or grain to all-purpose flour. Whole wheat flour produces a denser, coarser texture with a slightly nutty flavor; bran, rolled oats, and wheat germ give a chewy texture; and yellow cornmeal gives a grainy texture.

Superfine sugar and brown sugar (either light or dark) are equally suitable. The latter adds color and flavor to the muffins and making them slightly moister. Raw brown sugar is sometimes used to give the muffins a crunchy topping.

Use large eggs and, ideally, remove them from the refrigerator before using them to let them reach room temperature and prevent the mixture from curdling.

The liquid ingredient is variable and can range from milk, buttermilk, yogurt, sour cream, cream, coconut milk, and fruit juices or purees.

Oil and butter are interchangeable—butter gives the best flavor and texture, and oil makes the muffins moist. The advantage of oil is that it doesn't have to be melted and cooled first. Use sunflower oil for its mild flavor. The basic recipe uses 6 tablespoons of oil or melted butter, but this can be varied from as little as 4 tablespoons to as much as ½ cup, depending on preference. The richer the muffin, the longer it will stay fresh—low-fat muffins are best eaten freshly baked.

Additional Ingredients

Fresh fruits (for example berries, bananas, and apples) and dried fruits (such as raisins, golden raisins, cranberries, blueberries, apricots, dates, and prunes) are popular additions to muffins. Well-drained canned fruits are also suitable, as are frozen fruits, which should be used from frozen and not thawed.

Chocolate adds a touch of luxury—semisweet, milk, or white chocolate are all suitable in the form of chunks or chips. If using cocoa, then the quantity of flour should be reduced. Coffee gives a hint of sophistication.

Other ingredients that can be used to add flavor to muffins include nuts, which can be whole, slivered, chopped, or ground. Ground nuts are particularly good for adding moisture to the muffins. Choose from walnuts, pecan nuts, pine nuts, almonds, pistachios, peanuts, cashew nuts, macadamias, and hazelnuts. Try using seeds, too—for example, sesame, sunflower, pumpkin, and poppy seeds. Vary the type of nuts and seeds to give your muffins a personal touch.

It is also worth experimenting with spices (such as cinnamon, nutmeg, ginger, and cloves), citrus fruit rinds, extracts (such as vanilla and almond), and liqueurs (such as brandy, rum, or your favorite liqueur).

For savory muffins, cheeses, herbs, nuts, cooked meats, fish, and shellfish, as well as fresh, frozen, and canned vegetables, can be added. Grated zucchini, carrots, and chopped bell peppers are some favorites.

Top Tips for Perfect Muffins

- Preheat the oven and resist the temptation of opening the oven door during cooking.

- Measure out the ingredients accurately, using the appropriate measuring cups and spoons.

- Don't be tempted to add more baking powder, thinking the muffins will rise more. Too much will cause them to rise too much and then collapse, and the muffins will be heavy. They will also taste unpleasant.

- Don't overmix the batter because this will cause the muffins to be tough with a compact texture. The ingredients should just be moistened and the mixture lumpy with still a few traces of flour.

- Once you've made the batter, bake it immediately because the baking powder starts to work as soon as the liquid has been added to the flour (by relaxing the dough and causing it to rise).

- Do not overbake the muffins because they will become dry.

- Muffins are best eaten freshly baked or on the day they are made but, if necessary, they can be stored in an airtight container. To serve warm, reheat in the oven at 300°F/150°C for 5–10 minutes, or in the microwave on HIGH for 20–30 seconds.

- Muffins are perfect for freezing. Thaw at room temperature for 2–3 hours, or reheat frozen muffins on a baking tray at 350°F/180°C for 15–20 minutes.

Basic Muffin Mix

Makes 12 standard or 48 mini muffins

* oil or melted butter, for greasing (if using)
* 2 cups all-purpose flour
    (you may substitute whole wheat flour, bran, rolled oats, oatmeal, wheat germ, or cornmeal for up to half of this quantity)
* 1 tbsp baking powder
* ½ tsp baking soda, if using yogurt
* ⅛ tsp salt
* heaping ½ cup superfine sugar or firmly packed brown sugar (for savory muffins, just omit the sugar)
* 2 large eggs
* 1 cup milk
    (recipes may substitute buttermilk, yogurt, sour cream, cream, coconut milk, fruit juice, or fruit puree)
* 6 tbsp sunflower oil or melted, cooled butter
* 1 tsp vanilla extract

This is the basic recipe that all 100 variations of muffin in this book are based on.

For each recipe the basic mix is highlighted (*) for easy reference, so that all you have to do is follow the easy steps each time and a world of delicious and delectable muffins will await you.

Please note the basic ingredients may vary from time to time so please check these carefully.

Indulgent

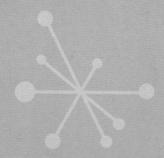

Chocolate Chunk Muffins

1. Preheat the oven to 400°F/200°C. Grease a 12-cup muffin pan or line with 12 muffin paper liners. Sift together the flour, baking powder, and salt into a large bowl. Stir in the sugar and chocolate chunks.

2. Lightly beat the eggs in a large pitcher or bowl, then beat in the milk, oil, and vanilla extract.

3. Make a well in the center of the dry ingredients and pour in the beaten liquid ingredients. Stir gently until just combined; do not overmix.

4. Spoon the batter into the prepared muffin pan. Bake in the preheated oven for about 20 minutes, until well risen, golden brown, and firm to the touch.

5. Let the muffins cool in the pan for 5 minutes, then serve warm or transfer to a wire rack and let cool completely.

Makes 12

* oil or melted butter, for greasing (if using)
* 2 cups all-purpose flour
* 1 tbsp baking powder
* ⅛ tsp salt
* heaping ½ cup superfine sugar
  1 cup chocolate chunks
* 2 large eggs
* 1 cup milk
* 6 tbsp sunflower oil or melted, cooled butter
* 1 tsp vanilla extract

Moist Gingerbread Muffins

1. Preheat the oven to 400°F/200°C. Grease a 12-cup muffin pan or line with 12 muffin paper liners. Sift together the flour, baking powder, ground ginger, cinnamon, and salt into a large bowl. Stir in the sugar and preserved ginger.

2. Lightly beat the eggs in a large pitcher or bowl, then beat in the milk, oil, and corn syrup. Make a well in the center of the dry ingredients and pour in the beaten liquid ingredients. Stir gently until just combined; do not overmix.

3. Spoon the batter into the prepared muffin pan. Bake in the preheated oven for about 20 minutes, until well risen, golden brown, and firm to the touch.

4. Let the muffins cool in the pan for 5 minutes, then serve warm or transfer to a wire rack and let cool completely.

Makes 12

* oil or melted butter, for greasing (if using)
* 2 cups all-purpose flour
* 1 tbsp baking powder
  4 tsp ground ginger
  1½ tsp ground cinnamon
* ⅛ tsp salt
* heaping ½ cup firmly packed light brown sugar
  3 pieces preserved ginger in syrup, finely chopped
* 2 large eggs
  ¾ cup milk
* 6 tbsp sunflower oil or melted, cooled butter
  4 tbsp dark corn syrup

Sticky Toffee Muffins

1. Preheat the oven to 400°F/200°C. Grease a 12-cup muffin pan or line with 12 muffin paper liners. Put the dates and water in a food processor and blend to form a rough puree.

2. Sift together the flour, baking powder, and salt into a large bowl. Stir in the sugar.

3. Lightly beat the eggs in a large pitcher or bowl, then beat in the date puree and oil. Make a well in the center of the dry ingredients and pour in the beaten liquid ingredients. Stir gently until just combined; do not overmix.

4. Spoon the batter into the prepared muffin pan. Bake in the preheated oven for about 20 minutes, until golden brown and firm to the touch.

5. Let the muffins cool in the pan for 5 minutes, then serve warm or transfer to a wire rack and let cool completely. Spread a teaspoon of Dulce de Leche over the top of each muffin before serving.

Makes 12

* oil or melted butter, for greasing (if using)
  1½ cups pitted dates
  1 cup water
* 2 cups all-purpose flour
* 1 tbsp baking powder
* ⅛ tsp salt
* heaping ½ cup firmly packed dark brown sugar
* 2 large eggs
* 6 tbsp sunflower oil or melted, cooled butter
  4 tbsp Dulce de Leche (from a jar), to serve

Brandy & Apricot Muffins

1. Put the chopped apricots in a bowl, add the brandy, and let soak for 1 hour. Grease a 12-cup muffin pan or line with 12 muffin paper liners.

2. Preheat the oven to 400°F/200°C. Put the soaked apricots and brandy in a food processor and blend to form a rough puree.

3. Sift together the flour, baking powder, and salt into a large bowl. Stir in the sugar.

4. Lightly beat the eggs in a large pitcher or bowl, then beat in the apricot puree, buttermilk, and oil. Make a well in the center of the dry ingredients and pour in the beaten liquid ingredients. Stir gently until just combined; do not overmix.

5. Spoon the batter into the prepared muffin pan. Bake in the preheated oven for about 20 minutes, until well risen, golden brown, and firm to the touch.

6. Let the muffins cool in the pan for 5 minutes, then serve warm or transfer to a wire rack and let cool completely.

Makes 12

heaping ½ cup dried apricots, coarsely chopped

3 tbsp brandy

* oil or melted butter, for greasing (if using)
* 2 cups all-purpose flour
* 1 tbsp baking powder
* ⅛ tsp salt
* heaping ½ cup superfine sugar
* 2 large eggs

¾ cup buttermilk

* 6 tbsp sunflower oil or melted, cooled butter

Jelly Doughnut Muffins

1. Preheat the oven to 400°F/200°C. Grease a 12-cup muffin pan or line with 12 muffin paper liners. Sift together the flour, baking powder, and salt into a large bowl. Stir in the sugar.

2. Lightly beat the eggs in a large pitcher or bowl, then beat in the milk, oil, and vanilla extract. Make a well in the center of the dry ingredients and pour in the beaten liquid ingredients. Stir gently until just combined; do not overmix.

3. Spoon half the batter into the prepared muffin pan. Add a teaspoon of jelly to the center of each then spoon in the remaining batter. Bake in the preheated oven for about 20 minutes, until well risen, golden brown, and firm to the touch.

4. Meanwhile, make the topping. Melt the butter. Spread the sugar in a wide, shallow bowl. When the muffins are baked, let them cool in the pan for 5 minutes. Dip the tops of the muffins in the melted butter then roll in the sugar. Serve warm or transfer to a wire rack and let cool completely.

Makes 12

- oil or melted butter, for greasing (if using)
- 2 cups all-purpose flour
- 1 tbsp baking powder
- ⅛ tsp salt
- heaping ½ cup superfine sugar
- 2 large eggs
- scant 1 cup milk
- 6 tbsp sunflower oil or melted, cooled butter
- 1 tsp vanilla extract
- 4 tbsp strawberry jelly or raspberry jelly

For the topping
½ cup butter
heaping ¾ cup sugar

Marzipan Muffins

1. Preheat the oven to 400°F/200°C. Grease a 12-cup muffin pan or line with 12 muffin paper liners. Cut the marzipan into 12 equal-size pieces. Roll each piece into a ball, and then flatten with the palm of your hand, making sure that it is no larger than the muffin pans or paper liners.

2. Sift together the flour, baking powder, and salt into a large bowl. Stir in the sugar.

3. Lightly beat the eggs in a large pitcher or bowl, then beat in the milk, oil, and almond extract. Make a well in the center of the dry ingredients and pour in the beaten liquid ingredients. Stir gently until just combined; do not overmix.

4. Spoon half the batter into the prepared muffin pan. Place a piece of marzipan in the center of each then spoon in the remaining batter. Top each muffin with a whole blanched almond. Bake in the preheated oven for about 20 minutes, until well risen, golden brown, and firm to the touch.

5. Let the muffins cool in the pan for 5 minutes, then serve warm or transfer to a wire rack and let cool completely.

Makes 12

* oil or melted butter, for greasing (if using)
* 6 oz/175 g marzipan
* 2 cups all-purpose flour
* 1 tbsp baking powder
* ⅛ tsp salt
* heaping ½ cup superfine sugar
* 2 large eggs
* scant 1 cup milk
* 6 tbsp sunflower oil or melted, cooled butter
* 1 tsp almond extract
* 12 whole blanched almonds

Brandied Peach Muffins

1. Preheat the oven to 400°F/200°C. Grease a 12-cup muffin pan or line with 12 muffin paper liners. Drain and finely chop the peaches.

2. Sift together the flour, baking powder, and salt into a large bowl. Stir in the sugar.

3. Lightly beat the eggs in a large pitcher or bowl, then beat in the buttermilk, oil, brandy, and orange rind. Make a well in the center of the dry ingredients, pour in the beaten liquid ingredients, and add the chopped peaches. Stir gently until just combined; do not overmix.

4. Spoon the batter into the prepared muffin pan. Bake in the preheated oven for about 20 minutes, until well risen, golden brown, and firm to the touch.

5. Let the muffins cool in the pan for 5 minutes, then serve warm or transfer to a wire rack and let cool completely.

Makes 12

* oil or melted butter, for greasing (if using)
* 14 oz/400 g canned peaches in natural juice
* 2 cups all-purpose flour
* 1 tbsp baking powder
* ⅛ tsp salt
* heaping ½ cup superfine sugar
* 2 large eggs
* ¾ cup buttermilk
* 6 tbsp sunflower oil or melted, cooled butter
* 3 tbsp brandy
* finely grated rind of 1 orange

Caribbean Rum & Raisin Muffins

1. Put the raisins in a bowl, add the rum, and let soak for 1 hour. Grease a 12-cup muffin pan or line with 12 muffin paper liners.

2. Preheat the oven to 400°F/200°C. Sift together the flour, baking powder, and salt into a large bowl. Stir in the sugar.

3. Lightly beat the eggs in a large pitcher or bowl, then beat in the milk and oil. Make a well in the center of the dry ingredients, pour in the beaten liquid ingredients, and add the soaked raisins. Stir gently until just combined; do not overmix.

4. Spoon the batter into the prepared muffin pan. Bake in the preheated oven for about 20 minutes, until well risen, golden brown, and firm to the touch.

5. Let the muffins cool in the pan for 5 minutes, then serve warm or transfer to a wire rack and let cool completely.

Makes 12

1½ cups raisins

3 tbsp rum

✳ oil or melted butter, for greasing (if using)

✳ 2 cups all-purpose flour

✳ 1 tbsp baking powder

✳ ⅛ tsp salt

✳ heaping ½ cup firmly packed dark brown sugar

✳ 2 large eggs

scant 1 cup milk

✳ 6 tbsp sunflower oil or melted, cooled butter

Gooey Butterscotch Cream Muffins

1. Preheat the oven to 400°F/200°C. Grease a 12-cup muffin pan or line with 12 muffin paper liners. Put the butterscotch candies in a strong plastic bag and hit with a meat mallet or the end of a wooden rolling pin until finely crushed.

2. Sift together the flour, baking powder, and salt into a large bowl. Stir in the sugar and crushed candies.

3. Lightly beat the eggs in a large pitcher or bowl, then beat in the cream and oil. Make a well in the center of the dry ingredients and pour in the beaten liquid ingredients. Stir gently until just combined; do not overmix.

4. Spoon the batter into the prepared muffin pan. Bake in the preheated oven for about 20 minutes, until well risen, golden brown, and firm to the touch.

5. Let the muffins cool in the pan for 5 minutes, then serve warm or transfer to a wire rack and let cool completely.

Makes 12

* oil or melted butter, for greasing (if using)
* 5½ oz/150g hard butterscotch candies
* 2 cups all-purpose flour
* 1 tbsp baking powder
* ⅛ tsp salt
* heaping ½ cup firmly packed dark brown sugar
* 2 large eggs
* 1 cup heavy cream
* 6 tbsp sunflower oil or melted, cooled butter

Carrot Cake Muffins

1. Preheat the oven to 400°F/200°C. Grease a 12-cup muffin pan or line with 12 muffin paper liners. Sift together the flour, baking powder, salt, and apple pie spice into a large bowl. Stir in the sugar, grated carrots, walnuts, and golden raisins.

2. Lightly beat the eggs in a large pitcher or bowl, then beat in the milk, oil, orange rind, and orange juice. Make a well in the center of the dry ingredients and pour in the beaten liquid ingredients. Stir gently until just combined; do not overmix.

3. Spoon the batter into the prepared muffin pan. Bake in the preheated oven for about 20 minutes, until well risen, golden brown, and firm to the touch.

4. Let the muffins cool in the pan for 5 minutes, then transfer to a wire rack and let cool completely.

5. To make the frosting, put the cream cheese and butter in a bowl and sift in the confectioners' sugar. Beat together until light and fluffy. When the muffins are cold, spread the frosting on top of each, then decorate with strips of orange zest. Chill the muffins in the refrigerator until ready to serve.

Makes 12

* oil or melted butter, for greasing (if using)
* 2 cups all-purpose flour
* 1 tbsp baking powder
* ⅛ tsp salt
  1 tsp apple pie spice
* heaping ½ cup firmly packed dark brown sugar
  1 cup grated carrots
  ½ cup walnuts or pecan nuts, coarsely chopped
  ½ cup golden raisins
* 2 large eggs
  ¾ cup milk
* 6 tbsp sunflower oil
  finely grated rind and juice of 1 orange
  strips of orange zest, to decorate

For the frosting
⅓ cup soft cream cheese
3 tbsp butter
⅜ cup confectioners' sugar

Coffee & Cream Muffins

1. Preheat the oven to 400°F/200°C. Grease a 12-cup muffin pan or line with 12 muffin paper liners. Put the coffee powder and boiling water in a cup and stir until dissolved. Let cool.

2. Meanwhile, sift together the flour, baking powder, and salt into a large bowl. Stir in the brown sugar.

3. Lightly beat the eggs in a large pitcher or bowl, then beat in the cream, oil, and dissolved coffee. Make a well in the center of the dry ingredients and pour in the beaten liquid ingredients. Stir gently until just combined; do not overmix.

4. Spoon the batter into the prepared muffin pan. Bake in the preheated oven for about 20 minutes, until well risen and firm to the touch.

5. Let the muffins cool in the pan for 5 minutes, then transfer to a wire rack and let cool completely.

6. Just before serving, whip the cream until it holds its shape. Spoon a dollop of the cream on top of each muffin, dust lightly with cocoa, and top with a chocolate-covered coffee bean.

Makes 12

* oil or melted butter, for greasing (if using)
2 tbsp instant coffee powder
2 tbsp boiling water
* 2 cups all-purpose flour
* 1 tbsp baking powder
* ⅛ tsp salt
* heaping ½ cup firmly packed dark brown sugar
* 2 large eggs
scant 1 cup heavy cream
* 6 tbsp sunflower oil or melted, cooled butter

For the topping
1¼ cups heavy cream
unsweetened cocoa, for dusting
12 chocolate-covered coffee beans

Cream & Spice Muffins

1. Preheat the oven to 400°F/200°C. Grease a 12-cup muffin pan or line with 12 muffin paper liners. Sift together the flour, baking powder, cinnamon, allspice, nutmeg, and salt into a large bowl. Stir in the brown sugar.

2. Lightly beat the eggs in a large pitcher or bowl, then beat in the cream and oil. Make a well in the center of the dry ingredients and pour in the beaten liquid ingredients. Stir gently until just combined, do not overmix.

3. Spoon the batter into the prepared muffin pan. Bake in the preheated oven for about 20 minutes, until well risen, golden brown, and firm to the touch.

4. Let the muffins cool in the pan for 5 minutes, then serve warm or transfer to a wire rack and let cool completely. Dust with confectioners' sugar before serving.

Makes 12

* oil or melted butter, for greasing (if using)
* 2 cups all-purpose flour
* 1 tbsp baking powder
  1 tsp ground cinnamon
  ½ tsp ground allspice
  ¼ tsp freshly grated nutmeg
* ⅛ tsp salt
* heaping ½ cup firmly packed light brown sugar
* 2 large eggs
* 1 cup heavy cream
* 6 tbsp sunflower oil or melted, cooled butter
  confectioners' sugar, for dusting

Triple Chocolate Chip Muffins

1. Preheat the oven to 400°F/200°C. Grease a 12-cup muffin pan or line with 12 muffin paper liners. Sift together the flour, baking powder, and salt into a large bowl. Stir in the sugar and chocolate chips.

2. Lightly beat the eggs in a large pitcher or bowl, then beat in the sour cream, oil, and vanilla extract. Make a well in the center of the dry ingredients and pour in the beaten liquid ingredients. Stir gently until just combined; do not overmix.

3. Spoon the batter into the prepared muffin pan. Bake in the preheated oven for about 20 minutes, until well risen, golden brown, and firm to the touch.

4. Let the muffins cool in the pan for 5 minutes, then serve warm or transfer to a wire rack and let cool completely.

Makes 12

- oil or melted butter, for greasing (if using)
- 2 cups all-purpose flour
- 1 tbsp baking powder
- ⅛ tsp salt
- heaping ½ cup firmly packed light brown sugar
- heaping ¼ cup semisweet chocolate chips
- heaping ¼ cup milk chocolate chips
- heaping ¼ cup white chocolate chips
- 2 large eggs
- 1 cup sour cream
- 6 tbsp sunflower oil or melted, cooled butter
- 1 tsp vanilla extract

Marshmallow Muffins

1. Preheat the oven to 400°F/200°C. Grease a 12-cup muffin pan or line with 12 muffin paper liners. Using scissors, cut the marshmallows in half.

2. Sift together the flour, cocoa, baking powder, and salt into a large bowl. Stir in the sugar and marshmallows.

3. Lightly beat the eggs in a large pitcher or bowl, then beat in the milk and oil. Make a well in the center of the dry ingredients and pour in the beaten liquid ingredients. Stir gently until just combined; do not overmix.

4. Spoon the batter into the prepared muffin pan. Bake in the preheated oven for about 20 minutes, until well risen and firm to the touch.

5. Let the muffins cool in the pan for 5 minutes, then serve warm or transfer to a wire rack and let cool completely.

Makes 12

* oil or melted butter, for greasing (if using)
* 1 cup mini white marshmallows
* heaping 1½ cups all-purpose flour
* ½ cup unsweetened cocoa
* 1 tbsp baking powder
* ⅛ tsp salt
* heaping ½ cup firmly packed light brown sugar
* 2 large eggs
* 1 cup milk
* 6 tbsp sunflower oil or melted, cooled butter

Frosted Cream Cheese Muffins

1. Preheat the oven to 400°F/200°C. Grease a 12-cup muffin pan or line with 12 muffin paper liners. Put ½ cup of the cream cheese in a bowl. Sift in 1 tablespoon of the confectioners' sugar and beat together.

2. Sift together the flour, baking powder, and salt into a large bowl. Stir in the brown sugar.

3. Lightly beat the eggs in a large pitcher or bowl, then beat in the sour cream, oil, and lemon rind. Make a well in the center of the dry ingredients and pour in the beaten liquid ingredients. Stir gently until just combined; do not overmix.

4. Spoon half the batter into the prepared muffin pan. Add a spoonful of the cream cheese mixture to the center of each, then spoon in the remaining batter. Bake in the preheated oven for about 20 minutes, until well risen, golden brown, and firm to the touch.

5. Let the muffins cool in the pan for 5 minutes, then transfer to a wire rack and let cool completely.

6. To make the frosting, put the remaining cream cheese in a bowl and sift in the remaining confectioners' sugar. Add the lemon juice and beat well together. Spread the frosting on top of the muffins then chill in the refrigerator until ready to serve.

Makes 12

- oil or melted butter, for greasing (if using)
- 1 cup soft cream cheese
- ½ cup confectioners' sugar
- 2 cups all-purpose flour
- 1 tbsp baking powder
- ⅛ tsp salt
- heaping ½ cup firmly packed dark brown sugar
- 2 large eggs
- scant 1 cup sour cream
- 6 tbsp sunflower oil or melted, cooled butter
- finely grated rind of 1 lemon
- 2 tsp fresh lemon juice

Chocolate Fudge Muffins

1. Preheat the oven to 400°F/200°C. Grease a 12-cup muffin pan or line with 12 muffin paper liners. Sift together the flour, cocoa, baking powder, and salt into a large bowl. Stir in the sugar.

2. Lightly beat the eggs in a large pitcher or bowl, then beat in the sour cream, oil, and corn syrup. Make a well in the center of the dry ingredients and pour in the beaten liquid ingredients. Stir gently until just combined; do not overmix.

3. Spoon the batter into the prepared muffin pan. Bake in the preheated oven for about 20 minutes, until well risen and firm to the touch.

4. Let the muffins cool in the pan for 5 minutes, then serve warm or transfer to a wire rack and let cool completely.

Makes 12

- oil or melted butter, for greasing (if using)
- heaping 1½ cups all-purpose flour
- ½ cup unsweetened cocoa
- 1 tbsp baking powder
- ⅛ tsp salt
- heaping ½ cup firmly packed light brown sugar
- 2 large eggs
- scant 1 cup sour cream
- 6 tbsp sunflower oil or melted, cooled butter
- 3 tbsp corn syrup

Frosted Chocolate Orange Muffins

1. Preheat the oven to 400°F/200°C. Grease a 12-cup muffin pan or line with 12 muffin paper liners. Finely grate the rind from the oranges and squeeze the juice. Make up the juice to 1 cup with milk and add the orange rind.

2. Sift together the flour, cocoa, baking powder, and salt into a large bowl. Stir in the brown sugar and chocolate chips.

3. Lightly beat the eggs in a large pitcher or bowl, then beat in the milk and orange mixture and the oil. Make a well in the center of the dry ingredients and pour in the beaten liquid ingredients. Stir gently until just combined; do not overmix.

4. Spoon the batter into the prepared muffin pan. Bake in the preheated oven for about 20 minutes, until well risen and firm to the touch.

5. Let the muffins cool in the pan for 5 minutes, then transfer to a wire rack and let cool completely.

6. To make the frosting, break the chocolate into a heatproof bowl, add the butter and water, and stand the bowl over a saucepan of gently simmering water. Stir constantly, until melted. Remove from the heat, sift in the confectioners' sugar, and beat until smooth. While the frosting is still warm, spread it on top of the muffins, then decorate with strips of orange zest.

Makes 12

- oil or melted butter, for greasing (if using)
- 2 oranges
- about ½ cup milk
- heaping 1½ cups all-purpose flour
- ½ cup unsweetened cocoa
- 1 tbsp baking powder
- ⅛ tsp salt
- heaping ½ cup firmly packed light brown sugar
- 1 cup semisweet chocolate chips
- 2 large eggs
- 6 tbsp sunflower oil or melted, cooled butter
- strips of orange zest, to decorate

For the frosting
- 2 oz/55 g semisweet chocolate
- 2 tbsp butter
- 2 tbsp water
- 1½ cups confectioners' sugar

Chocolate Cream Muffins

1. Preheat the oven to 400°F/200°C. Grease a 12-cup muffin pan or line with 12 muffin paper liners. Sift together the flour, cocoa, baking powder, and salt into a large bowl. Stir in the sugar and chocolate chips.

2. Lightly beat the eggs in a large pitcher or bowl, then beat in the cream and oil. Make a well in the center of the dry ingredients and pour in the beaten liquid ingredients. Stir gently until just combined; do not overmix.

3. Spoon the batter into the prepared muffin pan. Bake in the preheated oven for about 20 minutes, until well risen and firm to the touch.

4. Let the muffins cool in the pan for 5 minutes, then serve warm or transfer to a wire rack and let cool completely.

Makes 12

* oil or melted butter, for greasing (if using)
- heaping 1½ cups all-purpose flour
- ½ cup unsweetened cocoa
* 1 tbsp baking powder
* ⅛ tsp salt
* heaping ½ cup firmly packed light brown sugar
- 1 cup white chocolate chips
* 2 large eggs
* 1 cup heavy cream
* 6 tbsp sunflower oil or melted, cooled butter

Dark Chocolate & Ginger Muffins

1. Preheat the oven to 400°F/200°C. Grease a 12-cup muffin pan or line with 12 muffin paper liners. Sift together the flour, cocoa, baking powder, ground ginger, and salt into a large bowl. Stir in the sugar and preserved ginger.

2. Lightly beat the eggs in a large pitcher or bowl, then beat in the milk, oil, and ginger syrup. Make a well in the center of the dry ingredients and pour in the beaten liquid ingredients. Stir gently until just combined; do not overmix.

3. Spoon the batter into the prepared muffin pan. Bake in the preheated oven for about 20 minutes, until well risen and firm to the touch.

4. Let the muffins cool in the pan for 5 minutes, then serve warm or transfer to a wire rack and let cool completely.

Makes 12

* oil or melted butter, for greasing (if using)

  heaping 1½ cups all-purpose flour

  ½ cup unsweetened cocoa

* 1 tbsp baking powder

  1 tbsp ground ginger

* ⅛ tsp salt

* heaping ½ cup firmly packed dark brown sugar

  3 pieces preserved ginger in syrup, finely chopped, plus 2 tbsp syrup from the jar

* 2 large eggs

* 1 cup milk

* 6 tbsp sunflower oil or melted, cooled butter

20

Mint Chocolate Chip Muffins

1. Preheat the oven to 400°F/200°C. Grease a 12-cup muffin pan or line with 12 muffin paper liners. Sift together the flour, baking powder, and salt into a large bowl. Stir in the superfine sugar and chocolate chips.

2. Lightly beat the eggs in a large pitcher or bowl, then beat in the milk, oil, peppermint extract, and food coloring, if using, to color the mixture a very subtle shade of green. Make a well in the center of the dry ingredients and pour in the beaten liquid ingredients. Stir gently until just combined; do not overmix.

3. Spoon the batter into the prepared muffin pan. Bake in the preheated oven for about 20 minutes, until well risen and firm to the touch.

4. Let the muffins cool in the pan for 5 minutes, then serve warm or transfer to a wire rack and let cool completely. Dust with confectioners' sugar before serving.

Makes 12

- ✳ oil or melted butter, for greasing (if using)
- ✳ 2 cups all-purpose flour
- ✳ 1 tbsp baking powder
- ✳ ⅛ tsp salt
- ✳ heaping ½ cup superfine sugar
-   1 cup semisweet chocolate chips
- ✳ 2 large eggs
- ✳ 1 cup milk
- ✳ 6 tbsp sunflower oil or melted, cooled butter
-   1 tsp peppermint extract
-   1–2 drops of green food coloring (optional)
-   confectioners' sugar, for dusting

21

Chocolate Cinnamon Muffins

1. Preheat the oven to 400°F/200°C. Grease a 12-cup muffin pan or line with 12 muffin paper liners. Sift together the flour, cocoa, baking powder, cinnamon, and salt into a large bowl. Stir in the sugar and chocolate chips.

2. Lightly beat the eggs in a large pitcher or bowl, then beat in the milk and oil. Make a well in the center of the dry ingredients and pour in the beaten liquid ingredients. Stir gently until just combined; do not overmix.

3. Spoon the batter into the prepared muffin pan. Bake in the preheated oven for about 20 minutes, until well risen and firm to the touch.

4. Let the muffins cool in the pan for 5 minutes, then serve warm or transfer to a wire rack and let cool completely.

Makes 12

* oil or melted butter, for greasing (if using)
* heaping 1½ cups all-purpose flour
* ½ cup unsweetened cocoa
* 1 tbsp baking powder
* ½ tsp ground cinnamon
* ⅛ tsp salt
* heaping ½ cup firmly packed light brown sugar
* 1 cup semisweet chocolate chips
* 2 large eggs
* 1 cup milk
* 6 tbsp sunflower oil or melted, cooled butter

22

Marbled Chocolate Muffins

1. Preheat the oven to 400°F/200°C. Grease a 12-cup muffin pan or line with 12 muffin paper liners. Sift together the flour, baking powder, and salt into a large bowl. Stir in the sugar.

2. Lightly beat the eggs in a large pitcher or bowl, then beat in the milk, oil, and vanilla extract. Make a well in the center of the dry ingredients and pour in the beaten liquid ingredients. Stir gently until just combined; do not overmix.

3. Divide the batter between 2 bowls. Sift the cocoa into one bowl and mix together. Using teaspoons, spoon the batters into the prepared muffin pan, alternating the chocolate batter and the plain batter.

4. Bake in the preheated oven for about 20 minutes, until well risen, golden brown, and firm to the touch.

5. Let the muffins cool in the pan for 5 minutes, then serve warm or transfer to a wire rack and let cool completely.

Makes 12

- oil or melted butter, for greasing (if using)
- 2 cups all-purpose flour
- 1 tbsp baking powder
- ⅛ tsp salt
- heaping ½ cup superfine sugar
- 2 large eggs
- 1 cup milk
- 6 tbsp sunflower oil or melted, cooled butter
- 1 tsp vanilla extract
- 2 tbsp unsweetened cocoa

Fruit & Nut

23

Moist Orange & Almond Muffins

1. Preheat the oven to 400°F/200°C. Grease a 12-cup muffin pan or line with 12 muffin paper liners. Finely grate the rind from the oranges and squeeze the juice. Make up the juice to 1 cup with the milk and add the orange rind.

2. Sift together the flour, baking powder, and salt into a large bowl. Stir in the superfine sugar and ground almonds.

3. Lightly beat the eggs in a large pitcher or bowl, then beat in the orange and milk mixture, oil, and almond extract. Make a well in the center of the dry ingredients and pour in the beaten liquid ingredients. Stir gently until just combined; do not overmix.

4. Spoon the batter into the prepared muffin pan. Sprinkle the raw brown sugar over the tops of the muffins. Bake in the preheated oven for about 20 minutes, until well risen, golden brown, and firm to the touch.

5. Let the muffins cool in the pan for 5 minutes, then serve warm or transfer to a wire rack and let cool completely.

Makes 12

* oil or melted butter, for greasing (if using)
  2 oranges
  about scant ½ cup milk
  heaping 1½ cups all-purpose flour
* 1 tbsp baking powder
* ⅛ tsp salt
* heaping ½ cup superfine sugar
  ½ cup ground almonds
* 2 large eggs
* 6 tbsp sunflower oil or melted, cooled butter
  ½ tsp almond extract
  3 tbsp raw brown sugar

24

Apricot & Banana Muffins

1. Preheat the oven to 400°F/200°C. Grease a 12-cup muffin pan or line with 12 muffin paper liners. Sift together the flour, baking powder, and salt into a large bowl. Stir in the sugar and dried apricots.

2. Mash the bananas and put in a pitcher. Make up the puree to 1 cup with milk.

3. Lightly beat the eggs in a large pitcher or bowl, then beat in the banana and milk mixture and the oil. Make a well in the center of the dry ingredients and pour in the beaten liquid ingredients. Stir gently until just combined; do not overmix.

4. Spoon the batter into the prepared muffin pan. Bake in the preheated oven for about 20 minutes, until well risen, golden brown, and firm to the touch.

5. Let the muffins cool in the pan for 5 minutes, then serve warm or transfer to a wire rack and let cool completely.

Makes 12

* oil or melted butter, for greasing (if using)
* 2 cups all-purpose flour
* 1 tbsp baking powder
* ⅛ tsp salt
* heaping ½ cup superfine sugar
  ⅓ cup plumped dried apricots, finely chopped
  2 bananas
  about ⅔ cup milk
* 2 large eggs
* 6 tbsp sunflower oil or melted, cooled butter

Walnut & Cinnamon Muffins

1. Preheat the oven to 400°F/200°C. Grease a 12-cup muffin pan or line with 12 muffin paper liners. Sift together the flour, baking powder, cinnamon, and salt into a large bowl. Stir in the sugar and walnuts.

2. Lightly beat the eggs in a large pitcher or bowl, then beat in the milk, oil, and vanilla extract. Make a well in the center of the dry ingredients and pour in the beaten liquid ingredients. Stir gently until just combined; do not overmix.

3. Spoon the batter into the prepared muffin pan. Bake in the preheated oven for about 20 minutes, until well risen, golden brown, and firm to the touch.

4. Let the muffins cool in the pan for 5 minutes, then serve warm or transfer to a wire rack and let cool completely.

Makes 12

* oil or melted butter, for greasing (if using)
* 2 cups all-purpose flour
* 1 tbsp baking powder
  1 tsp ground cinnamon
* ⅛ tsp salt
* heaping ½ cup firmly packed light brown sugar
  1 cup walnut pieces, coarsely chopped
* 2 large eggs
* 1 cup milk
* 6 tbsp sunflower oil or melted, cooled butter
* 1 tsp vanilla extract

Fresh Strawberry & Cream Muffins

1. Preheat the oven to 400°F/200°C. Grease a 12-cup muffin pan or line with 12 muffin paper liners. Chop the strawberries into small pieces.

2. Sift together the flour, baking powder, and salt into a large bowl. Stir in the sugar and chopped strawberries.

3. Lightly beat the eggs in a large pitcher or bowl, then beat in the light cream, oil, and vanilla extract. Make a well in the center of the dry ingredients and pour in the beaten liquid ingredients. Stir gently until just combined; do not overmix.

4. Spoon the batter into the prepared muffin pan. Bake in the preheated oven for about 20 minutes, until well risen, golden brown, and firm to the touch.

5. Let the muffins cool in the pan for 5 minutes, then transfer to a wire rack and let cool completely.

6. Whip the heavy cream until stiff. When the muffins are cold, pipe or spread the cream on top, then top each with a whole strawberry. Chill the muffins in the refrigerator until ready to serve.

Makes 12

- oil or melted butter, for greasing (if using)
- heaping 1 cup strawberries
- 2 cups all-purpose flour
- 1 tbsp baking powder
- ⅛ tsp salt
- heaping ½ cup superfine sugar
- 2 large eggs
- 1 cup light cream
- 6 tbsp sunflower oil or melted, cooled butter
- 1 tsp vanilla extract
- ½ cup heavy cream
- 12 whole small strawberries, to decorate

27

Blueberry Muffins

1. Preheat the oven to 400°F/200°C. Grease a 12-cup muffin pan or line with 12 muffin paper liners. Sift together the flour, baking powder, and salt into a large bowl. Stir in the sugar and blueberries.

2. Lightly beat the eggs in a large pitcher or bowl, then beat in the milk, oil, vanilla extract, and lemon rind. Make a well in the center of the dry ingredients and pour in the beaten liquid ingredients. Stir gently until just combined; do not overmix.

3. Spoon the batter into the prepared muffin pan. Bake in the preheated oven for about 20 minutes, until well risen, golden brown, and firm to the touch.

4. Let the muffins cool in the pan for 5 minutes, then serve warm or transfer to a wire rack and let cool completely.

Makes 12

- oil or melted butter, for greasing (if using)
- 2 cups all-purpose flour
- 1 tbsp baking powder
- ⅛ tsp salt
- heaping ½ cup firmly packed light brown sugar
- scant 1½ cups frozen blueberries
- 2 large eggs
- 1 cup milk
- 6 tbsp sunflower oil or melted, cooled butter
- 1 tsp vanilla extract
- finely grated rind of 1 lemon

Orange, Walnut & Rosemary Muffins

1. Preheat the oven to 400°F/200°C. Grease a 12-cup muffin pan or line with 12 muffin paper liners. Sift together the flour, baking powder, baking soda, and salt into a large bowl. Stir in the superfine sugar and walnuts.

2. Lightly beat the eggs in a large pitcher or bowl, then beat in the yogurt, oil, orange rind, and chopped rosemary leaves. Make a well in the center of the dry ingredients and pour in the beaten liquid ingredients. Stir gently until just combined; do not overmix.

3. Spoon the batter into the prepared muffin pan. Bake in the preheated oven for about 20 minutes, until well risen, golden brown, and firm to the touch.

4. Let the muffins cool in the pan for 5 minutes, then transfer to a wire rack and let cool completely.

5. When the muffins are cold, make the frosting. Sift the confectioners' sugar into a bowl. Add the orange rind and orange juice and stir until the mixture is smooth and thick enough to coat the back of a wooden spoon.

6. Spoon the frosting on top of each muffin. Decorate with a rosemary sprig and let set for about 30 minutes before serving.

Makes 12

- oil or melted butter, for greasing (if using)
- 2 cups all-purpose flour
- 1 tbsp baking powder
- ½ tsp baking soda
- ⅛ tsp salt
- heaping ⅓ cup superfine sugar
- heaping ½ cup walnut pieces, coarsely chopped
- 2 large eggs
- 1 cup plain yogurt
- 6 tbsp sunflower oil or melted, cooled butter
- finely grated rind of 2 oranges
- 1 tbsp finely chopped fresh rosemary leaves, plus extra sprigs to decorate

For the frosting
1½ cups confectioners' sugar
finely grated rind of ½ orange
3–4 tsp fresh orange juice

Lemon & Poppy Seed Muffins

1. Preheat the oven to 400°F/200°C. Grease a 12-cup muffin pan or line with 12 muffin paper liners. Sift together the flour, baking powder, and salt into a large bowl. Stir in the sugar and poppy seeds.

2. Lightly beat the eggs in a large pitcher or bowl, then beat in the milk, oil, and lemon rind. Make a well in the center of the dry ingredients and pour in the beaten liquid ingredients. Stir gently until just combined; do not overmix.

3. Spoon the batter into the prepared muffin pan. Bake in the preheated oven for about 20 minutes, until well risen, golden brown, and firm to the touch.

4. Let the muffins cool in the pan for 5 minutes, then serve warm or transfer to a wire rack and let cool completely.

Makes 12

* oil or melted butter, for greasing (if using)
* 2 cups all-purpose flour
* 1 tbsp baking powder
* ⅛ tsp salt
* heaping ½ cup superfine sugar
  2 tbsp poppy seeds
* 2 large eggs
* 1 cup milk
* 6 tbsp sunflower oil or melted, cooled butter
  finely grated rind of 2 lemons

Apple Streusel Muffins

1. Preheat the oven to 400°F/200°C. Grease a 12-cup muffin pan or line with 12 muffin paper liners.

2. To make the streusel topping, put the flour and cinnamon into a bowl. Cut the butter into small pieces, add to the bowl with the flour, and rub it in with your fingertips until the mixture resembles fine breadcrumbs. Stir in the sugar and set aside.

3. To make the muffins, sift together the flour, baking powder, cinnamon, and salt into a large bowl. Stir in the sugar. Peel, core, and finely chop the apple. Add to the flour mixture and stir together.

4. Lightly beat the eggs in a large pitcher or bowl, then beat in the milk and oil. Make a well in the center of the dry ingredients and pour in the beaten liquid ingredients. Stir gently until just combined; do not overmix.

5. Spoon the batter into the prepared muffin pan. Scatter the topping over each muffin. Bake in the preheated oven for about 20 minutes, until well risen, golden brown, and firm to the touch.

6. Let the muffins cool in the pan for 5 minutes, then serve warm or transfer to a wire rack and let cool completely.

Makes 12

* oil or melted butter, for greasing (if using)
* 2 cups all-purpose flour
* 1 tbsp baking powder
  ½ tsp ground cinnamon
* ⅛ tsp salt
* heaping ½ cup firmly packed light brown sugar
  9 oz/250 g baking apple
* 2 large eggs
* 1 cup milk
* 6 tbsp sunflower oil or melted, cooled butter

For the streusel topping
½ cup all-purpose flour
¼ tsp ground cinnamon
3 tbsp butter
2 tbsp light brown sugar

Maple Pecan Muffins

1. Preheat the oven to 400°F/200°C. Grease a 12-cup muffin pan or line with 12 muffin paper liners. Sift together the flour, baking powder, and salt into a large bowl. Stir in the sugar and pecan nuts.

2. Lightly beat the eggs in a large pitcher or bowl, then beat in the buttermilk, 1/3 cup maple syrup, and the oil. Make a well in the center of the dry ingredients and pour in the beaten liquid ingredients. Stir gently until just combined; do not overmix.

3. Spoon the batter into the prepared muffin pan. Top each muffin with a pecan nut half. Bake in the preheated oven for about 20 minutes, until well risen, golden brown, and firm to the touch.

4. Let the muffins cool in the pan for 5 minutes, then brush the tops with the remaining maple syrup to glaze. Serve warm or transfer to a wire rack and let cool completely.

Makes 12

* oil or melted butter, for greasing (if using)
* 2 cups all-purpose flour
* 1 tbsp baking powder
* 1/8 tsp salt
* heaping 1/2 cup superfine sugar
  1 cup pecan nuts, coarsely chopped
* 2 large eggs
  3/4 cup buttermilk
  1/3 cup maple syrup, plus 3 tbsp extra for glazing
* 6 tbsp sunflower oil or melted, cooled butter
  12 pecan nut halves

Spicy Dried Fruit Muffins

1. Preheat the oven to 400°F/200°C. Grease a 12-cup muffin pan or line with 12 muffin paper liners. Sift together the flour, baking powder, apple pie spice, and salt into a large bowl. Stir in the sugar and mixed dried fruit.

2. Lightly beat the eggs in a large pitcher or bowl, then beat in the milk and oil. Make a well in the center of the dry ingredients and pour in the beaten liquid ingredients. Stir gently until just combined; do not overmix.

3. Spoon the batter into the prepared muffin pan. Bake in the preheated oven for about 20 minutes, until well risen, golden brown, and firm to the touch.

4. Let the muffins cool in the pan for 5 minutes, then serve warm or transfer to a wire rack and let cool completely.

Makes 12

* oil or melted butter, for greasing (if using)
* 2 cups all-purpose flour
* 1 tbsp baking powder
  1 tbsp apple pie spice
* ⅛ tsp salt
* heaping ½ cup superfine sugar
  heaping 1 cup mixed dried fruit
* 2 large eggs
* 1 cup milk
* 6 tbsp sunflower oil or melted, cooled butter

33

Hazelnut & Coffee Muffins

1. Preheat the oven to 400°F/200°C. Grease a 12-cup muffin pan or line with 12 muffin paper liners. Put the coffee powder and boiling water in a cup and stir until dissolved. Let cool.

2. Meanwhile, finely chop ⅔ cup of the hazelnuts and coarsely chop the remaining nuts. Sift together the flour, baking powder, and salt into a large bowl. Stir in the sugar and finely chopped hazelnuts.

3. Lightly beat the eggs in a large pitcher or bowl, then beat in the buttermilk, oil, and dissolved coffee. Make a well in the center of the dry ingredients and pour in the beaten liquid ingredients. Stir gently until just combined; do not overmix.

4. Spoon the batter into the prepared muffin pan. Scatter the reserved coarsely chopped hazelnuts over the top of each muffin. Bake in the preheated oven for about 20 minutes, until well risen, golden brown, and firm to the touch.

5. Let the muffins cool in the pan for 5 minutes, then serve warm or transfer to a wire rack and let cool completely.

Makes 12

- oil or melted butter, for greasing (if using)
- 2 tbsp instant coffee powder
- 2 tbsp boiling water
- heaping 1 cup hazelnuts
- 2 cups all-purpose flour
- 1 tbsp baking powder
- ⅛ tsp salt
- heaping ½ cup firmly packed light brown sugar
- 2 large eggs
- scant 1 cup buttermilk
- 6 tbsp sunflower oil or melted, cooled butter

Cherry & Coconut Muffins

1. Preheat the oven to 400°F/200°C. Grease a 12-cup muffin pan or line with 12 muffin paper liners. Cut the candied cherries into small pieces.

2. Sift together the flour, baking powder, and salt into a large bowl. Stir in the sugar, coconut, and chopped candied cherries.

3. Lightly beat the eggs in a large pitcher or bowl, then beat in the coconut milk, oil, and vanilla extract. Make a well in the center of the dry ingredients and pour in the beaten liquid ingredients. Stir gently until just combined; do not overmix.

4. Spoon the batter into the prepared muffin pan. Top each muffin with a whole fresh cherry. Bake in the preheated oven for about 20 minutes, until well risen, golden brown, and firm to the touch.

5. Let the muffins cool in the pan for 5 minutes, then serve warm or transfer to a wire rack and let cool completely.

Makes 12

* oil or melted butter, for greasing (if using)
  heaping ½ cup candied cherries
* 2 cups all-purpose flour
* 1 tbsp baking powder
* ⅛ tsp salt
* heaping ½ cup superfine sugar
  scant ½ cup dry unsweetened coconut
* 2 large eggs
* 1 cup coconut milk
* 6 tbsp sunflower oil or melted, cooled butter
* 1 tsp vanilla extract
  12 whole fresh cherries on their stalks

Sour Cream & Pineapple Muffins

1. Preheat the oven to 400°F/200°C. Grease a 12-cup muffin pan or line with 12 muffin paper liners. Drain and finely chop the pineapple slices.

2. Sift together the flour, baking powder, and salt into a large bowl. Stir in the sugar and chopped pineapple.

3. Lightly beat the eggs in a large pitcher or bowl, then beat in the sour cream, oil, pineapple juice, and vanilla extract. Make a well in the center of the dry ingredients and pour in the beaten liquid ingredients. Stir gently until just combined; do not overmix.

4. Spoon the batter into the prepared muffin pan. Bake in the preheated oven for about 20 minutes, until well risen, golden brown, and firm to the touch.

5. Let the muffins cool in the pan for 5 minutes, then serve warm or transfer to a wire rack and let cool completely.

Makes 12

- oil or melted butter, for greasing (if using)
- 2 slices canned pineapple in natural juice, plus 2 tbsp juice from the can
- 2 cups all-purpose flour
- 1 tbsp baking powder
- ⅛ tsp salt
- heaping ½ cup superfine sugar
- 2 large eggs
- scant 1 cup sour cream
- 6 tbsp sunflower oil or melted, cooled butter
- 1 tsp vanilla extract

Mini Orange & Cardamom Muffins

1 Preheat the oven to 400°F/200°C. Grease two 24-cup mini muffin pans or line with 48 mini muffin paper liners. Finely grate the rind from the oranges and squeeze the juice. Make up the juice to 1 cup with the milk and add the orange rind.

2 Remove the seeds from the cardamom pods and crush finely. Sift together the flour, baking powder, and salt into a large bowl. Stir in the sugar and crushed cardamom seeds.

3 Lightly beat the eggs in a large pitcher or bowl, then beat in the orange and milk mixture and the oil. Make a well in the center of the dry ingredients and pour in the beaten liquid ingredients. Stir gently until just combined; do not overmix.

4 Spoon the batter into the prepared muffin pans. Bake in the preheated oven for about 20 minutes, until well risen, golden brown, and firm to the touch.

5 Let the muffins cool in the pans for 5 minutes, then serve warm or transfer to a wire rack and let cool completely.

Makes 48

* oil or melted butter, for greasing (if using)
2 oranges
about scant ½ cup milk
6 cardamom pods
* 2 cups all-purpose flour
* 1 tbsp baking powder
* ⅛ tsp salt
* heaping ½ cup superfine sugar
* 2 large eggs
* 6 tbsp sunflower oil or melted, cooled butter

Raspberry Crumble Muffins

1. Preheat the oven to 400°F/200°C. Grease a 12-cup muffin pan or line with 12 muffin paper liners.

2. To make the crumble topping, put the flour into a bowl. Cut the butter into small pieces, add to the bowl with the flour, and rub it in with your fingertips until the mixture resembles fine breadcrumbs. Stir in the sugar and set aside.

3. To make the muffins, sift together the flour, baking powder, baking soda, and salt into a large bowl. Stir in the sugar.

4. Lightly beat the eggs in a large pitcher or bowl, then beat in the yogurt, oil, and vanilla extract. Make a well in the center of the dry ingredients, pour in the beaten liquid ingredients, and add the raspberries. Stir gently until just combined; do not overmix.

5. Spoon the batter into the prepared muffin pan. Scatter the crumble topping over each muffin and press down lightly. Bake in the preheated oven for about 20 minutes, until well risen, golden brown, and firm to the touch.

6. Let the muffins cool in the pan for 5 minutes, then serve warm or transfer to a wire rack and let cool completely.

Makes 12

- oil or melted butter, for greasing (if using)
- 2 cups all-purpose flour
- 1 tbsp baking powder
- ½ tsp baking soda
- ⅛ tsp salt
- heaping ½ cup superfine sugar
- 2 large eggs
- 1 cup plain yogurt
- 6 tbsp sunflower oil or melted, cooled butter
- 1 tsp vanilla extract
- scant 1 cup frozen raspberries

For the crumble topping
- ½ cup all-purpose flour
- 3 tbsp butter
- 2 tbsp superfine sugar

38

Buttermilk Berry Muffins

1. Preheat the oven to 400°F/200°C. Grease a 12-cup muffin pan or line with 12 muffin paper liners. Cut any large berries, such as strawberries, into small pieces.

2. Sift together the flour, baking powder, and salt into a large bowl. Stir in the superfine sugar.

3. Lightly beat the eggs in a large pitcher or bowl, then beat in the buttermilk, oil, and vanilla extract. Make a well in the center of the dry ingredients, pour in the beaten liquid ingredients, and add the berries. Stir gently until just combined; do not overmix.

4. Spoon the batter into the prepared muffin pan. Bake in the preheated oven for about 20 minutes, until well risen, golden brown, and firm to the touch.

5. Let the muffins cool in the pan for 5 minutes, then serve warm or transfer to a wire rack and let cool completely. Dust with confectioners' sugar before serving.

Makes 12

- oil or melted butter, for greasing (if using)
- scant 1 cup frozen mixed berries, such as blueberries, raspberries, blackberries, and strawberries
- 2 cups all-purpose flour
- 1 tbsp baking powder
- ⅛ tsp salt
- heaping ½ cup superfine sugar
- 2 large eggs
- 1 cup buttermilk
- 6 tbsp sunflower oil or melted, cooled butter
- 1 tsp vanilla extract
- confectioners' sugar, for dusting

39

Tropical Banana & Passion Fruit Muffins

1. Preheat the oven to 400°F/200°C. Grease a 12-cup muffin pan or line with 12 muffin paper liners. Mash the bananas and put in a pitcher. Make up the puree to 1 cup with milk.

2. Sift together the flour, baking powder, and salt into a large bowl. Stir in the sugar.

3. Lightly beat the eggs in a large pitcher or bowl, then beat in the banana and milk mixture, oil, and vanilla extract. Make a well in the center of the dry ingredients and pour in the beaten liquid ingredients. Stir gently until just combined; do not overmix.

4. Spoon the batter into the prepared muffin pan. Bake in the preheated oven for about 20 minutes, until well risen, golden brown, and firm to the touch.

5. Let the muffins cool in the pan for 5 minutes, then transfer to a wire rack and let cool completely.

6. Meanwhile, halve the passion fruits and spoon the pulp into a small saucepan. Add the honey and heat very gently until warmed through. Spoon on top of the muffins before serving.

Makes 12

* oil or melted butter, for greasing (if using)
2 bananas
about ⅔ cup milk
* 2 cups all-purpose flour
* 1 tbsp baking powder
* ⅛ tsp salt
* heaping ½ cup firmly packed light brown sugar
* 2 large eggs
* 6 tbsp sunflower oil or melted, cooled butter
* 1 tsp vanilla extract
2 passion fruits
2 tbsp clear honey

40

Toasted Almond & Apricot Muffins

1. Cut the apricots into small pieces and put in a bowl. Add the orange juice and let soak for 1 hour. Grease a 12-cup muffin pan or line with 12 muffin paper liners.

2. Meanwhile, line a broiler pan with a sheet of foil and spread out the blanched almonds. Toast under the broiler until golden brown, turning frequently. When cool enough to handle, coarsely chop the almonds.

3. Preheat the oven to 400°F/200°C. Sift together the flour, baking powder, and salt into a large bowl. Stir in the sugar and chopped almonds.

4. Lightly beat the eggs in a large pitcher or bowl, then beat in the buttermilk, oil, and almond extract. Make a well in the center of the dry ingredients, pour in the beaten liquid ingredients, and add the soaked apricots. Stir gently until just combined; do not overmix.

5. Spoon the batter into the prepared muffin pan. Scatter the slivered almonds on top of each muffin. Bake in the preheated oven for about 20 minutes, until well risen, golden brown, and firm to the touch.

6. Let the muffins cool in the pan for 5 minutes, then serve warm or transfer to a wire rack and let cool completely.

Makes 12

heaping ½ cup dried apricots
3 tbsp fresh orange juice
oil or melted butter,
   for greasing (if using)
⅓ cup blanched almonds
2 cups all-purpose flour
1 tbsp baking powder
⅛ tsp salt
heaping ½ cup superfine sugar
2 large eggs
scant 1 cup buttermilk
6 tbsp sunflower oil or melted,
   cooled butter
¼ tsp almond extract
heaping ⅓ cup slivered
   almonds

41

Blackberry & Apple Muffins

1. Preheat the oven to 400°F/200°C. Grease a 12-cup muffin pan or line with 12 muffin paper liners. Sift together the flour, baking powder, and salt into a large bowl. Stir in the light brown sugar. Peel, core, and finely chop the apple. Add to the flour mixture and stir together.

2. Lightly beat the eggs in a large pitcher or bowl, then beat in the buttermilk, oil, and vanilla extract. Make a well in the center of the dry ingredients, pour in the beaten liquid ingredients, and add the blackberries. Stir gently until just combined; do not overmix.

3. Spoon the batter into the prepared muffin pan. Sprinkle the raw brown sugar over the tops of the muffins. Bake in the preheated oven for about 20 minutes, until well risen, golden brown, and firm to the touch.

4. Let the muffins cool in the pan for 5 minutes, then serve warm or transfer to a wire rack and let cool completely.

Makes 12

* oil or melted butter, for greasing (if using)
* 2 cups all-purpose flour
* 1 tbsp baking powder
* ⅛ tsp salt
* heaping ½ cup firmly packed light brown sugar
* 9 oz/250 g apple
* 2 large eggs
* 1 cup buttermilk
* 6 tbsp sunflower oil or melted, cooled butter
* 1 tsp vanilla extract
* scant 1½ cups frozen blackberries
* 3 tbsp raw brown sugar

Crunchy Peanut Butter Muffins

1. Preheat the oven to 400°F/200°C. Grease a 12-cup muffin pan or line with 12 muffin paper liners. To make the topping, finely chop the peanuts. Put in a bowl, add the raw brown sugar, mix together, and set aside.

2. Sift together the flour, baking powder, and salt into a large bowl. Stir in the dark brown sugar.

3. Lightly beat the eggs in a large pitcher or bowl, then beat in the milk, oil, and peanut butter. Make a well in the center of the dry ingredients and pour in the beaten liquid ingredients. Stir gently until just combined; do not overmix.

4. Spoon the batter into the prepared muffin pan. Sprinkle the peanut topping over the muffins. Bake in the preheated oven for about 20 minutes, until well risen, golden brown, and firm to the touch.

5. Let the muffins cool in the pan for 5 minutes, then serve warm or transfer to a wire rack and let cool completely.

Makes 12

* oil or melted butter, for greasing (if using)
* 2 cups all-purpose flour
* 1 tbsp baking powder
* ⅛ tsp salt
* heaping ½ cup firmly packed dark brown sugar
* 2 large eggs
  ¾ cup milk
* 6 tbsp sunflower oil or melted, cooled butter
  heaping ½ cup crunchy peanut butter

For the peanut topping
⅓ cup unsalted roasted peanuts
3 tbsp raw brown sugar

Cranberry & Almond Muffins

1. Preheat the oven to 400°F/200°C. Grease a 12-cup muffin pan or line with 12 muffin paper liners. Sift together the flour, baking powder, and salt into a large bowl. Stir in the superfine sugar and ground almonds.

2. Lightly beat the eggs in a large pitcher or bowl, then beat in the buttermilk, oil, and almond extract. Make a well in the center of the dry ingredients, pour in the beaten liquid ingredients, and add the cranberries. Stir gently until just combined; do not overmix.

3. Spoon the batter into the prepared muffin pan. Sprinkle the slivered almonds and raw brown sugar over the tops of the muffins. Bake in the preheated oven for about 20 minutes, until well risen, golden brown, and firm to the touch.

4. Let the muffins cool in the pan for 5 minutes, then serve warm or transfer to a wire rack and let cool completely.

Makes 12

* oil or melted butter, for greasing (if using)
* heaping 1½ cups all-purpose flour
* 1 tbsp baking powder
* ⅛ tsp salt
* heaping ½ cup superfine sugar
* ½ cup ground almonds
* 2 large eggs
* 1 cup buttermilk
* 6 tbsp sunflower oil or melted, cooled butter
* ½ tsp almond extract
* scant 1½ cups fresh or frozen cranberries
* heaping ⅓ cup slivered almonds
* 3 tbsp raw brown sugar

Citrus Fruit Muffins

① Preheat the oven to 400°F/200°C. Grease a 12-cup muffin pan or line with 12 muffin paper liners. Sift together the flour, baking powder, baking soda, and salt into a large bowl. Stir in the superfine sugar.

② Lightly beat the eggs in a large pitcher or bowl, then beat in the yogurt, oil, and all the citrus rinds. Make a well in the center of the dry ingredients and pour in the beaten liquid ingredients. Stir gently until just combined; do not overmix.

③ Spoon the batter into the prepared muffin pan. Bake in the preheated oven for about 20 minutes, until well risen, golden brown, and firm to the touch.

④ Let the muffins cool in the pan for 5 minutes, then transfer to a wire rack and let cool completely.

⑤ To make the frosting, put the butter and cream cheese in a large bowl and, using an electric mixer, beat together until smooth. Sift the confectioners' sugar into the mixture, then beat together until well mixed. Gradually beat in the citrus juice, adding enough to form a spreading consistency. When the muffins are cold, spread the frosting on top of each, then decorate with strips of citrus zest. Chill the muffins in the refrigerator until ready to serve.

Makes 12

* oil or melted butter, for greasing (if using)
* 2 cups all-purpose flour
* 1 tbsp baking powder
* ½ tsp baking soda
* ⅛ tsp salt
* heaping ½ cup superfine sugar
* 2 large eggs
* 1 cup plain yogurt
* 6 tbsp sunflower oil or melted, cooled butter

finely grated rind of 1 lemon
finely grated rind of 1 lime
finely grated rind of 1 orange
strips of citrus zest, to decorate

For the frosting
2 tbsp butter
½ cup soft cream cheese
1 cup confectioners' sugar
1 tsp fresh lemon, lime, or orange juice

Celebratory

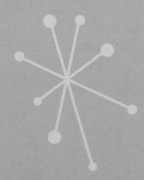

Happy Birthday Muffins

1. Preheat the oven to 400°F/200°C. Grease a 12-cup muffin pan or line with 12 muffin paper liners. Sift together the flour, baking powder, and salt into a large bowl. Stir in the superfine sugar.

2. Lightly beat the eggs in a large pitcher or bowl, then beat in the milk, oil, and lemon rind. Make a well in the center of the dry ingredients and pour in the beaten liquid ingredients. Stir gently until just combined; do not overmix.

3. Spoon the batter into the prepared muffin pan. Bake in the preheated oven for about 20 minutes, until well risen, golden brown, and firm to the touch.

4. Let the muffins cool in the pan for 5 minutes, then transfer to a wire rack and let cool completely.

5. To make the frosting, put the butter in a large bowl and beat until fluffy. Sift in the confectioners' sugar and beat together until smooth and creamy.

6. When the muffins are cold, spread each one with a little of the frosting, then place a candleholder and candle on top.

Makes 12

- ✳ oil or melted butter, for greasing (if using)
- ✳ 2 cups all-purpose flour
- ✳ 1 tbsp baking powder
- ✳ ⅛ tsp salt
- ✳ heaping ½ cup superfine sugar
- ✳ 2 large eggs
- ✳ 1 cup milk
- ✳ 6 tbsp sunflower oil or melted, cooled butter

finely grated rind of 1 lemon

12 candles and candleholders, to decorate

For the frosting

6 tbsp butter, softened

1½ cups confectioners' sugar

46

Valentine Heart Muffins

1. To make the marzipan hearts, dust a work surface with confectioners' sugar, then roll out the marzipan to a thickness of ¼ inch/5 mm. Using a small heart-shaped cutter, cut out 12 hearts. Line a tray with waxed paper, dust with confectioners' sugar, and place the hearts on it. Let dry for 3–4 hours.

2. Preheat the oven to 400°F/200°C. Grease a 12-cup heart-shaped muffin pan. Sift together the flour, cocoa, baking powder, and salt into a large bowl. Stir in the brown sugar.

3. Lightly beat the eggs in a large pitcher or bowl, then beat in the buttermilk and oil. Make a well in the center of the dry ingredients and pour in the beaten liquid ingredients. Stir gently until just combined; do not overmix.

4. Spoon the batter into the prepared muffin pan. Bake in the preheated oven for about 20 minutes, until well risen and firm to the touch.

5. Let the muffins cool in the pan for 5 minutes, then transfer to a wire rack and let cool completely.

6. To make the frosting, melt the chocolate in a heatproof bowl set over a pan of gently simmering water. Put the butter in a large bowl and beat until fluffy. Sift in the confectioners' sugar and beat together until smooth and creamy. Add the melted chocolate and beat together. Spread the frosting on top of the muffins, then decorate each with a marzipan heart.

Makes 12

* oil or melted butter, for greasing

heaping 1½ cups all-purpose flour

½ cup unsweetened cocoa

* 1 tbsp baking powder

* ⅛ tsp salt

* heaping ½ cup firmly packed light brown sugar

* 2 large eggs

* 1 cup buttermilk

* 6 tbsp sunflower oil or melted, cooled butter

For the marzipan hearts
confectioners' sugar, for dusting

70 g/2½ oz marzipan, colored with a few drops of red food coloring

For the frosting
2 oz/55 g semisweet chocolate

½ cup butter, softened

2 cups confectioners' sugar

Christmas Snowflake Muffins

1. Preheat the oven to 400°F/200°C. Grease a 12-cup muffin pan or line with 12 muffin paper liners. Sift together the flour, baking powder, allspice, and salt into a large bowl. Stir in the brown sugar.

2. Lightly beat the eggs in a large pitcher or bowl, then beat in the milk and oil. Make a well in the center of the dry ingredients, pour in the beaten liquid ingredients, and add the mincemeat. Stir gently until just combined; do not overmix.

3. Spoon the batter into the prepared muffin pan. Bake in the preheated oven for about 20 minutes, until well risen, golden brown, and firm to the touch.

4. Let the muffins cool in the pan for 5 minutes, then transfer to a wire rack and let cool completely.

5. Knead the fondant icing until pliable. On a surface dusted with confectioners' sugar, roll out the fondant icing to a thickness of ¼ inch/5 mm. Using a 3-inch/7-cm fluted cutter, cut out 12 "snowflakes."

6. Heat the jam until runny, then brush it over the tops of the muffins. Place a snowflake on top, then decorate with silver dragées.

Makes 12

* oil or melted butter, for greasing (if using)
* 2 cups all-purpose flour
* 1 tbsp baking powder
* 1 tsp allspice
* ⅛ tsp salt
* heaping ½ cup firmly packed dark brown sugar
* 2 large eggs
* scant ½ cup milk
* 6 tbsp sunflower oil or melted, cooled butter
* ⅔ cup luxury mincemeat with candied cherries and nuts
* 1 lb/450 g fondant icing
* confectioners' sugar, for dusting
* 2½ tsp apricot jam
* silver dragées, to decorate

Easter Muffins

1. Preheat the oven to 400°F/200°C. Grease a 12-cup muffin pan or line with 12 muffin paper liners. Sift together the flour, cocoa, baking powder, and salt into a large bowl. Stir in the brown sugar.

2. Lightly beat the eggs in a large pitcher or bowl, then beat in the buttermilk and oil. Make a well in the center of the dry ingredients and pour in the beaten liquid ingredients. Stir gently until just combined; do not overmix.

3. Spoon the batter into the prepared muffin pan. Bake in the preheated oven for about 20 minutes, until well risen and firm to the touch.

4. Let the muffins cool in the pan for 5 minutes, then transfer to a wire rack and let cool completely.

5. To make the frosting, put the butter in a large bowl and beat until fluffy. Sift in the confectioners' sugar and beat together until smooth and creamy, then beat in the milk.

6. When the muffins are cold, put the frosting in a pastry bag with a large star tip attached, and pipe a circle around the top of each muffin to form a "nest." Place chocolate eggs in the center of each nest to decorate.

Makes 12

* oil or melted butter, for greasing (if using)

heaping 1½ cups all-purpose flour

½ cup unsweetened cocoa

* 1 tbsp baking powder
* ⅛ tsp salt
* heaping ½ cup firmly packed light brown sugar
* 2 large eggs
* 1 cup buttermilk
* 6 tbsp sunflower oil or melted, cooled butter

For the frosting
6 tbsp butter, softened

1½ cups confectioners' sugar

1 tbsp milk

9 oz/250 g sugar-coated mini chocolate eggs, to decorate

49

Anniversary Muffins

1. Preheat the oven to 400°F/200°C. Grease a 12-cup muffin pan or line with 12 muffin paper liners. Sift together the flour, baking powder, and salt into a large bowl. Stir in the superfine sugar.

2. Lightly beat the eggs in a large pitcher or bowl, then beat in the buttermilk, oil, and lemon rind. Make a well in the center of the dry ingredients and pour in the beaten liquid ingredients. Stir gently until just combined; do not overmix.

3. Spoon the batter into the prepared muffin pan. Bake in the preheated oven for about 20 minutes, until well risen, golden brown, and firm to the touch.

4. Let the muffins cool in the pan for 5 minutes, then transfer to a wire rack and let cool completely.

5. To make the frosting, put the butter in a large bowl and beat until fluffy. Sift in the confectioners' sugar and beat together until smooth and creamy.

6. When the muffins are cold, put the frosting in a pastry bag with a large star tip attached, and pipe circles on top of each muffin to cover the top. Sprinkle with the gold or silver dragées to decorate.

Makes 12

* oil or melted butter, for greasing (if using)
* 2 cups all-purpose flour
* 1 tbsp baking powder
* ⅛ tsp salt
* heaping ½ cup superfine sugar
* 2 large eggs
* 1 cup buttermilk
* 6 tbsp sunflower oil or melted, cooled butter
* finely grated rind of 1 lemon
* gold or silver dragées, to decorate

For the frosting
6 tbsp butter, softened
1½ cups confectioners' sugar

Baby Shower Muffins

① Preheat the oven to 400°F/200°C. Grease a 12-cup muffin pan or line with 12 muffin paper liners. Sift together the flour, baking powder, and salt into a large bowl. Stir in the superfine sugar.

② Lightly beat the eggs in a large pitcher or bowl, then beat in the buttermilk, oil, and lemon rind. Make a well in the center of the dry ingredients and pour in the beaten liquid ingredients. Stir gently until just combined; do not overmix.

③ Spoon the batter into the prepared muffin pan. Bake in the preheated oven for about 20 minutes, until well risen, golden brown, and firm to the touch.

④ Let the muffins cool in the pan for 5 minutes, then transfer to a wire rack and let cool completely.

⑤ When the muffins are cold, make the frosting. Sift the confectioners' sugar into a bowl. Add the water and stir until the mixture is smooth and thick enough to coat the back of a wooden spoon. Add 1 or 2 drops of food coloring and stir into the frosting until it is evenly colored pink or pale blue.

⑥ Spoon the frosting on top of each muffin. Top with a sugared almond and let set for about 30 minutes before serving.

Makes 12

※ oil or melted butter, for greasing (if using)
✳ 2 cups all-purpose flour
✳ 1 tbsp baking powder
✳ ⅛ tsp salt
✳ heaping ½ cup superfine sugar
✳ 2 large eggs
✳ 1 cup buttermilk
✳ 6 tbsp sunflower oil or melted, cooled butter
finely grated rind of 1 lemon
12 pink or blue sugared almonds, to decorate

For the frosting
1½ cups confectioners' sugar
3–4 tsp hot water
1–2 drops of red or blue food coloring

Rose-Topped Wedding Muffins

1. Preheat the oven to 400°F/200°C. Increase the quantity of ingredients according to the number of wedding guests invited, working in double quantities to make 24 muffins each time. Grease the appropriate number of muffin pans or line with muffin paper liners. Sift together the flour, baking powder, and salt into a large bowl. Stir in the superfine sugar.

2. Lightly beat the eggs in a large pitcher or bowl, then beat in the milk, oil, and vanilla extract. Make a well in the center of the dry ingredients and pour in the beaten liquid ingredients. Stir gently until just combined; do not overmix.

3. Spoon the batter into the prepared muffin pans. Bake in the preheated oven for about 20 minutes, until well risen, golden brown, and firm to the touch.

4. Let the muffins cool in the pans for 5 minutes, then transfer to a wire rack and let cool completely. Store the muffins in the freezer until required.

5. On the day of serving, if using fresh flowers, rinse and let dry on paper towels. For the frosting, sift the confectioners' sugar into a bowl. Add the water and stir until the mixture is smooth and thick enough to coat the back of a wooden spoon. Spoon the frosting on top of each muffin, then top with a sugar rose, rose petal, or rose bud.

Makes 12

* oil or melted butter, for greasing (if using)
* 2 cups all-purpose flour
* 1 tbsp baking powder
* ⅛ tsp salt
* heaping ½ cup superfine sugar
* 2 large eggs
* 1 cup milk
* 6 tbsp sunflower oil or melted, cooled butter
* 1 tsp vanilla extract
  12 store-bought sugar roses or fresh rose petals or buds, to decorate

For the frosting
1½ cups confectioners' sugar
3–4 tsp hot water

52

Halloween Pumpkin Muffins

1. Preheat the oven to 400°F/200°C. Grease a 12-cup muffin pan or line with 12 muffin paper liners. Sift together the flour, baking powder, pumpkin pie spice, and salt into a large bowl. Stir in the sugar.

2. Lightly beat the eggs in a large pitcher or bowl, then beat in the milk and oil. Make a well in the center of the dry ingredients, pour in the beaten liquid ingredients, and add the pumpkin flesh. Stir gently until just combined; do not overmix.

3. Spoon the batter into the prepared muffin pan. Bake in the preheated oven for about 20 minutes, until well risen, golden brown, and firm to the touch.

4. Let the muffins cool in the pan for 5 minutes, then serve warm or transfer to a wire rack and let cool completely. Spread a teaspoon of Dulce de Leche over the top of each muffin before serving.

Makes 12

* oil or melted butter, for greasing (if using)
* 2 cups all-purpose flour
* 1 tbsp baking powder
  1 tsp pumpkin pie spice
* ⅛ tsp salt
* heaping ½ cup firmly packed dark brown sugar
* 2 large eggs
  scant 1 cup milk
* 6 tbsp sunflower oil or melted, cooled butter
  15 oz/425 g canned pumpkin flesh
  4 tbsp Dulce de Leche (from a jar)

Fresh Flower Muffins

① Preheat the oven to 400°F/200°C. Grease a 12-cup muffin pan or line with 12 muffin paper liners. Carefully wash the flower heads and let dry on paper towels.

② Sift together the flour, baking powder, and salt into a large bowl. Stir in the superfine sugar

③ Lightly beat the eggs in a large pitcher or bowl, then beat in the buttermilk, oil, and lemon rind. Make a well in the center of the dry ingredients and pour in the beaten liquid ingredients. Stir gently until just combined; do not overmix.

④ Spoon the batter into the prepared muffin pan. Bake in the preheated oven for about 20 minutes, until well risen, golden brown, and firm to the touch.

⑤ Let the muffins cool in the pan for 5 minutes, then transfer to a wire rack and let cool completely.

⑥ To make the frosting, put the butter in a large bowl and beat until fluffy. Sift in the confectioners' sugar and beat together until smooth and creamy. When the muffins are cold, put the frosting in a pastry bag with a large star tip attached, and pipe circles on top of each muffin to cover the top. Before serving, place a flower head on top to decorate.

Makes 12

✳ oil or melted butter, for greasing (if using)

12 edible flower heads, such as lavender, nasturtiums, violets, primroses, or roses, to decorate

✳ 2 cups all-purpose flour

✳ 1 tbsp baking powder

✳ ⅛ tsp salt

✳ heaping ½ cup superfine sugar

✳ 2 large eggs

✳ 1 cup buttermilk

✳ 6 tbsp sunflower oil or melted, cooled butter

finely grated rind of 1 lemon

For the frosting
6 tbsp butter, softened
1½ cups confectioners' sugar

Thanksgiving Cranberry & Orange Muffins

1. Put the cranberries in a bowl, add the orange juice, and let soak for 1 hour. Grease a 12-cup muffin pan or line with 12 muffin paper liners.

2. Preheat the oven to 400°F/200°C. Sift together the flour, baking powder, and salt into a large bowl. Stir in the sugar.

3. Lightly beat the eggs in a large pitcher or bowl, then beat in the milk, oil, and orange rind. Make a well in the center of the dry ingredients, pour in the beaten liquid ingredients, and add the soaked cranberries. Stir gently until just combined; do not overmix.

4. Spoon the batter into the prepared muffin pan. Bake in the preheated oven for about 20 minutes, until well risen, golden brown, and firm to the touch.

5. Let the muffins cool in the pan for 5 minutes, then serve warm or transfer to a wire rack and let cool completely.

Makes 12

scant 1½ cups dried cranberries

3 tbsp fresh orange juice

* oil or melted butter, for greasing (if using)

* 2 cups all-purpose flour

* 1 tbsp baking powder

* ⅛ tsp salt

* heaping ½ cup superfine sugar

* 2 large eggs

scant 1 cup milk

* 6 tbsp sunflower oil or melted, cooled butter

finely grated rind of 1 orange

55

Children's Party Muffins

① Preheat the oven to 400°F/200°C. Grease a 12-cup muffin pan or line with 12 muffin paper liners. Sift together the flour, baking powder, and salt into a large bowl. Stir in the superfine sugar.

② Lightly beat the eggs in a large pitcher or bowl, then beat in the milk, oil, and vanilla extract. Make a well in the center of the dry ingredients and pour in the beaten liquid ingredients. Stir gently until just combined; do not overmix.

③ Spoon the batter into the prepared muffin pan. Bake in the preheated oven for about 20 minutes, until well risen, golden brown, and firm to the touch.

④ Let the muffins cool in the pan for 5 minutes, then serve warm or transfer to a wire rack and let cool completely.

⑤ When the muffins are cold, make the frosting. Sift the confectioners' sugar into a bowl. Add the water and stir until the mixture is smooth and thick enough to coat the back of a wooden spoon. Spoon the frosting on top of each muffin, then add the decoration of your choice. Let set for about 30 minutes before serving.

Makes 12

* oil or melted butter, for greasing (if using)
* 2 cups all-purpose flour
* 1 tbsp baking powder
* ⅛ tsp salt
* heaping ½ cup superfine sugar
* 2 large eggs
* 1 cup milk
* 6 tbsp sunflower oil or melted, cooled butter
* 1 tsp vanilla extract
  a variety of small candies, to decorate

For the frosting
1½ cups confectioners' sugar
3–4 tsp hot water

Rocky Road Chocolate Muffins

1. Preheat the oven to 400°F/200°C. Grease a 12-cup muffin pan or line with 12 muffin paper liners. Sift together the flour, cocoa, baking powder, and salt into a large bowl. Stir in the sugar, chocolate chips, and marshmallows.

2. Lightly beat the eggs in a large pitcher or bowl, then beat in the milk and oil. Make a well in the center of the dry ingredients and pour in the beaten liquid ingredients. Stir gently until just combined; do not overmix.

3. Spoon the batter into the prepared muffin pan. Bake in the preheated oven for about 20 minutes, until risen and firm to the touch.

4. Let the muffins cool in the pan for 5 minutes, then serve warm or transfer to a wire rack and let cool completely.

Makes 12

* oil or melted butter, for greasing (if using)

heaping 1½ cups all-purpose flour

½ cup unsweetened cocoa

* 1 tbsp baking powder
* ⅛ tsp salt
* heaping ½ cup superfine sugar

heaping ½ cup white chocolate chips

½ cup white mini marshmallows, cut in half

* 2 large eggs
* 1 cup milk
* 6 tbsp sunflower oil or melted, cooled butter

Malted Chocolate Muffins

1. Preheat the oven to 400°F/200°C. Grease a 12-cup muffin pan or line with 12 muffin paper liners. Coarsely crush the chocolate balls, reserving 12 whole ones to decorate.

2. Sift together the flour, cocoa, baking powder, and salt into a large bowl. Stir in the sugar and crushed chocolate balls.

3. Lightly beat the eggs in a large pitcher or bowl, then beat in the buttermilk and oil. Make a well in the center of the dry ingredients and pour in the beaten liquid ingredients. Stir gently until just combined; do not overmix.

4. Spoon the batter into the prepared muffin pan. Bake in the preheated oven for about 20 minutes, until well risen and firm to the touch.

5. Let the muffins cool in the pan for 5 minutes, then transfer to a wire rack and let cool completely.

6. To make the frosting, melt the chocolate in a heatproof bowl set over a pan of gently simmering water. Remove from the heat. Put the butter in a large bowl and beat until fluffy. Sift in the confectioners' sugar and beat together until smooth and creamy. Add the melted chocolate and beat together until well mixed. Spread the frosting on top of the muffins and decorate each with one of the reserved chocolate balls.

Makes 12

* oil or melted butter, for greasing (if using)
* 5½ oz/150g malted chocolate balls
* heaping 1½ cups all-purpose flour
* ½ cup unsweetened cocoa
* 1 tbsp baking powder
* ⅛ tsp salt
* heaping ½ cup firmly packed light brown sugar
* 2 large eggs
* 1 cup buttermilk
* 6 tbsp sunflower oil or melted, cooled butter

For the frosting
2 oz/55 g semisweet chocolate
½ cup butter, softened
2 cups confectioners' sugar

58

Mother's Day Breakfast Muffins

1. Preheat the oven to 400°F/200°C. Grease a 12-cup muffin pan or line with 12 muffin paper liners. Sift together the flour, baking powder, and salt into a large bowl. Stir in the superfine sugar.

2. Lightly beat the eggs in a large pitcher or bowl, then beat in the milk, oil, and orange extract. Make a well in the center of the dry ingredients and pour in the beaten liquid ingredients. Stir gently until just combined; do not overmix.

3. Spoon the batter into the prepared muffin pan. Bake in the preheated oven for about 20 minutes, until well risen, golden brown, and firm to the touch.

4. Let the muffins cool in the pan for 5 minutes. Meanwhile, arrange the strawberries in a bowl and pour the juice into a glass.

5. Dust the tops of the muffins with confectioners' sugar. Serve warm with the strawberries and juice.

Makes 12

* oil or melted butter, for greasing (if using)
* 2 cups all-purpose flour
* 1 tbsp baking powder
* ⅛ tsp salt
* heaping ½ cup superfine sugar
* 2 large eggs
* 1 cup milk
* 6 tbsp sunflower oil or melted, cooled butter
* 1 tsp orange extract
* fresh strawberries and fruit juice, to serve
* confectioners' sugar, for dusting

59

Decadent Chocolate Dessert Muffins

1. Preheat the oven to 400°F/200°C. Grease a 12-cup muffin pan. Sift together the flour, cocoa, baking powder, and salt into a large bowl. Stir in the sugar.

2. Lightly beat the eggs in a large pitcher or bowl, then beat in the cream and oil. Make a well in the center of the dry ingredients and pour in the beaten liquid ingredients. Stir gently until just combined; do not overmix.

3. Break the chocolate evenly into 12 squares. Spoon half the batter into the prepared muffin pan, place a piece of chocolate in the center of each, then spoon in the remaining batter. Bake in the preheated oven for about 20 minutes, until well risen and firm to the touch.

4. Meanwhile, make the sauce. Melt the chocolate and butter together in a heatproof bowl set over a pan of gently simmering water. Stir until blended then stir in the cream and mix together. Remove from the heat and stir until smooth.

5. Let the muffins cool in the pan for 5 minutes, then remove from the pan and place on serving plates. Serve warm with the chocolate sauce poured over the top.

Makes 12

* oil or melted butter, for greasing
* heaping 1½ cups all-purpose flour
* ½ cup unsweetened cocoa
* 1 tbsp baking powder
* ⅛ tsp salt
* heaping ½ cup firmly packed light brown sugar
* 2 large eggs
* 1 cup light cream
* 6 tbsp sunflower oil or melted, cooled butter
* 3 oz/85 g semisweet chocolate

For the sauce
* 7 oz/200 g semisweet chocolate
* 2 tbsp butter
* ¼ cup light cream

60

After Dinner Coffee Liqueur Muffins

1. Preheat the oven to 400°F/200°C. Grease a 12-cup muffin pan or line with 12 muffin paper liners. Put the coffee powder and boiling water in a cup and stir until dissolved. Let cool.

2. Meanwhile, sift together the flour, baking powder, and salt into a large bowl. Stir in the light brown sugar.

3. Lightly beat the eggs in a large pitcher or bowl, then beat in the milk, oil, dissolved coffee, and liqueur. Make a well in the center of the dry ingredients and pour in the beaten liquid ingredients. Stir gently until just combined; do not overmix.

4. Spoon the batter into the prepared muffin pan. Sprinkle the raw brown sugar over the tops of the muffins. Bake in the preheated oven for about 20 minutes, until well risen, golden brown, and firm to the touch.

5. Let the muffins cool in the pan for 5 minutes, then serve warm or transfer to a wire rack and let cool completely.

Makes 12

* oil or melted butter, for greasing (if using)
* 2 tbsp instant coffee powder
* 2 tbsp boiling water
* 2 cups all-purpose flour
* 1 tbsp baking powder
* ⅛ tsp salt
* heaping ½ cup firmly packed light brown sugar
* 2 large eggs
* scant ½ cup milk
* 6 tbsp sunflower oil or melted, cooled butter
* 6 tbsp coffee liqueur
* 3 tbsp raw brown sugar

Savory

61

Cornmeal Muffins

1. Preheat the oven to 400°F/200°C. Grease a 12-cup muffin pan or line with 12 muffin paper liners. Sift together the flour, baking powder, salt, and pepper to taste into a large bowl. Stir in the cornmeal.

2. Lightly beat the eggs in a large pitcher or bowl, then beat in the milk and oil. Make a well in the center of the dry ingredients, pour in the beaten liquid ingredients, and add the corn. Stir gently until just combined; do not overmix.

3. Spoon the batter into the prepared muffin pan. Bake in the preheated oven for about 20 minutes, until well risen, golden brown, and firm to the touch.

4. Let the muffins cool in the pan for 5 minutes, then serve warm.

Makes 12

* oil or melted butter, for greasing (if using)
* 1¼ cups all-purpose flour
* 1 tbsp baking powder
* ⅛ tsp salt
* freshly ground black pepper
* ¾ cup yellow cornmeal
* 2 large eggs
* 1 cup milk
* 6 tbsp sunflower oil or melted, cooled butter
* 1 cup frozen corn kernels

62

Cheese & Ham Muffins

1. Preheat the oven to 400°F/200°C. Grease a 12-cup muffin pan or line with 12 muffin paper liners. Sift together the flour, baking powder, salt, and pepper to taste into a large bowl. Stir in the ham and a scant 1 cup of the cheddar cheese.

2. Lightly beat the eggs in a large pitcher or bowl, then beat in the milk and oil. Make a well in the center of the dry ingredients and pour in the beaten liquid ingredients. Stir gently until just combined; do not overmix.

3. Spoon the batter into the prepared muffin pan. Scatter the remaining cheese over the tops of the muffins. Bake in the preheated oven for about 20 minutes, until well risen, golden brown, and firm to the touch.

4. Let the muffins cool in the pan for 5 minutes, then serve warm.

Makes 12

* oil or melted butter, for greasing (if using)
* 2 cups all-purpose flour
* 1 tbsp baking powder
* ⅛ tsp salt
  freshly ground black pepper
  3½ oz/100 g sliced ham, finely chopped
  1¼ cups coarsely grated sharp cheddar cheese
* 2 large eggs
* 1 cup milk
* 6 tbsp sunflower oil or melted, cooled butter

Mini Bleu Cheese & Pear Muffins

1. Preheat the oven to 400°F/200°C. Grease two 24-cup mini muffin pans or line with 48 mini muffin paper liners. Chop the pears into small pieces. Sift together the flour, baking powder, salt, and pepper to taste into a large bowl. Stir in the bleu cheese and pears.

2. Lightly beat the eggs in a large pitcher or bowl, then beat in the milk and oil. Make a well in the center of the dry ingredients and pour in the beaten liquid ingredients. Stir gently until just combined; do not overmix.

3. Spoon the batter into the prepared muffin pan. Scatter the walnuts over the tops of the muffins. Bake in the preheated oven for about 20 minutes, until well risen, golden brown, and firm to the touch.

4. Let the muffins cool in the pan for 5 minutes, then serve warm.

Makes 48

* oil or melted butter, for greasing (if using)
* 14 oz/400 g canned pear halves in natural juice, drained
* 2 cups all-purpose flour
* 1 tbsp baking powder
* ⅛ tsp salt
* freshly ground black pepper
* heaping ¾ cup finely crumbled bleu cheese, such as Stilton or Gorgonzola
* 2 large eggs
* 1 cup milk
* 6 tbsp sunflower oil or melted, cooled butter
* heaping ¼ cup walnut pieces

Brie & Cranberry Muffins

1. Preheat the oven to 400°F/200°C. Grease a 12-cup muffin pan or line with 12 muffin paper liners. Sift together the flour, baking powder, baking soda, salt, and pepper to taste into a large bowl. Stir in the Brie.

2. Lightly beat the eggs in a large pitcher or bowl, then beat in the yogurt and oil. Make a well in the center of the dry ingredients and pour in the beaten liquid ingredients. Stir gently until just combined; do not overmix.

3. Spoon half the batter into the prepared muffin pan. Add a teaspoon of cranberry jelly to the center of each, then spoon in the remaining batter. Bake in the preheated oven for about 20 minutes, until well risen, golden brown, and firm to the touch.

4. Let the muffins cool in the pan for 5 minutes, then serve warm.

Makes 12

* oil or melted butter, for greasing (if using)
* 2 cups all-purpose flour
* 1 tbsp baking powder
* ½ tsp baking soda
* ⅛ tsp salt
  freshly ground black pepper
  5½ oz/150 g Brie, chilled and finely cubed
* 2 large eggs
* 1 cup plain yogurt
* 6 tbsp sunflower oil or melted, cooled butter
  4 tbsp cranberry jelly

65

Crumble-Topped Cheese & Chive Muffins

1. Preheat the oven to 400°F/200°C. Grease a 12-cup muffin pan or line with 12 muffin paper liners. To make the crumble topping, put the flour into a bowl. Cut the butter into small pieces, add to the bowl with the flour, then rub it in with your fingertips until the mixture resembles fine breadcrumbs. Stir in the cheddar cheese and season to taste with salt and pepper.

2. To make the muffins, sift together the flour, baking powder, salt, and pepper to taste into a large bowl. Stir in the cheddar cheese and chives.

3. Lightly beat the eggs in a large pitcher or bowl, then beat in the buttermilk and oil. Make a well in the center of the dry ingredients and pour in the beaten liquid ingredients. Stir gently until just combined; do not overmix.

4. Spoon the batter into the prepared muffin pan. Scatter the topping over the tops of each muffin. Bake in the preheated oven for about 20 minutes, until well risen, golden brown, and firm to the touch.

5. Let the muffins cool in the pan for 5 minutes, then serve warm.

Makes 12

* oil or melted butter, for greasing (if using)
* 2 cups all-purpose flour
* 1 tbsp baking powder
* 1/8 tsp salt
  freshly ground black pepper
  1 1/3 cups coarsely grated sharp cheddar cheese
  4 tbsp snipped fresh chives
* 2 large eggs
* 1 cup buttermilk
* 6 tbsp sunflower oil or melted, cooled butter

For the crumble topping
1/2 cup all-purpose flour

3 tbsp butter

1/4 cup coarsely grated cheddar cheese

salt and pepper

Parmesan & Pine Nut Muffins

1. Preheat the oven to 400°F/200°C. Grease a 12-cup muffin pan or line with 12 muffin paper liners. To make the topping, mix together the Parmesan cheese and pine nuts and set aside.

2. To make the muffins, sift together the flour, baking powder, salt, and pepper to taste into a large bowl. Stir in the Parmesan cheese and pine nuts.

3. Lightly beat the eggs in a large pitcher or bowl, then beat in the buttermilk and oil. Make a well in the center of the dry ingredients and pour in the beaten liquid ingredients. Stir gently until just combined; do not overmix.

4. Spoon the batter into the prepared muffin pan. Scatter the topping over the muffins. Bake in the preheated oven for about 20 minutes, until well risen, golden brown, and firm to the touch.

5. Let the muffins cool in the pan for 5 minutes, then serve warm.

Makes 12

* oil or melted butter, for greasing (if using)
* 2 cups all-purpose flour
* 1 tbsp baking powder
* ⅛ tsp salt
  freshly ground black pepper
  ¾ cup freshly grated Parmesan cheese
  ½ cup pine nuts
* 2 large eggs
* 1 cup buttermilk
* 6 tbsp sunflower oil or melted, cooled butter

For the topping
4 tsp freshly grated Parmesan cheese
¼ cup pine nuts

Cream Cheese & Garlic Muffins

① Preheat the oven to 400°F/200°C. Grease a 12-cup muffin pan or line with 12 muffin paper liners. Sift together the flour, baking powder, baking soda, salt, and pepper to taste into a large bowl.

② Lightly beat the eggs in a large pitcher or bowl, then beat in the yogurt, oil, and cream cheese until smooth. Make a well in the center of the dry ingredients and pour in the beaten liquid ingredients. Stir gently until just combined; do not overmix.

③ Spoon the batter into the prepared muffin pan. Bake in the preheated oven for about 20 minutes, until well risen, golden brown, and firm to the touch.

④ Let the muffins cool in the pan for 5 minutes, then serve warm.

Makes 12

※ oil or melted butter, for greasing (if using)
※ 2 cups all-purpose flour
※ 1 tbsp baking powder
※ ½ tsp baking soda
※ ⅛ tsp salt
　 freshly ground black pepper
※ 2 large eggs
　 ⅔ cup plain yogurt
※ 6 tbsp sunflower oil or melted, cooled butter
　 ¾ cup soft cream cheese flavored with garlic and herbs

68

Scallion & Goat Cheese Muffins

1. Preheat the oven to 400°F/200°C. Grease a 12-cup muffin pan or line with 12 muffin paper liners. Sift together the flour, baking powder, salt, and pepper to taste into a large bowl. Stir in the scallions and goat cheese.

2. Lightly beat the eggs in a large pitcher or bowl, then beat in the buttermilk and oil. Make a well in the center of the dry ingredients and pour in the beaten liquid ingredients. Stir gently until just combined; do not overmix.

3. Spoon the batter into the prepared muffin pan. Bake in the preheated oven for about 20 minutes, until well risen, golden brown, and firm to the touch.

4. Let the muffins cool in the pan for 5 minutes, then serve warm.

Makes 12

* oil or melted butter, for greasing (if using)
* 2 cups all-purpose flour
* 1 tbsp baking powder
* ⅛ tsp salt
  freshly ground black pepper
  1 bunch scallions, finely sliced
  5½ oz/150g goat cheese, finely diced
* 2 large eggs
* 1 cup buttermilk
* 6 tbsp sunflower oil or melted, cooled butter

Smoked Salmon & Dill Muffins

1. Preheat the oven to 400°F/200°C. Grease a 12-cup muffin pan or line with 12 muffin paper liners. Sift together the flour, baking powder, salt, and pepper to taste into a large bowl.

2. Lightly beat the eggs in a large pitcher or bowl, then beat in the buttermilk and oil. Make a well in the center of the dry ingredients, pour in the beaten liquid ingredients, and add the chopped smoked salmon and chopped dill. Stir gently until just combined; do not overmix.

3. Spoon the batter into the prepared muffin pan. Bake in the preheated oven for about 20 minutes, until well risen, golden brown, and firm to the touch.

4. Let the muffins cool in the pan for 5 minutes, then serve warm. Serve garnished with small strips of smoked salmon and sprigs of dill.

Makes 12

* oil or melted butter, for greasing (if using)
* 2 cups all-purpose flour
* 1 tbsp baking powder
* ⅛ tsp salt
  freshly ground black pepper
* 2 large eggs
* 1 cup buttermilk
* 6 tbsp sunflower oil or melted, cooled butter
  5½ oz/150g smoked salmon, finely chopped, plus extra to garnish
  2 tbsp chopped fresh dill, plus extra sprigs to garnish

Mini Shrimp & Parsley Muffins

1. Preheat the oven to 400°F/200°C. Grease two 24-cup mini muffin pans or line with 48 mini muffin paper liners. Chop the shrimp into small pieces. Sift together the flour, baking powder, salt, and pepper to taste into a large bowl. Stir in the chopped shrimp.

2. Lightly beat the eggs in a large pitcher or bowl, then beat in the buttermilk, oil, and parsley. Make a well in the center of the dry ingredients and pour in the beaten liquid ingredients. Stir gently until just combined; do not overmix.

3. Spoon the batter into the prepared muffin pans. Bake in the preheated oven for about 20 minutes, until well risen, golden brown, and firm to the touch.

4. Let the muffins cool in the pans for 5 minutes, then serve warm.

Makes 48

- oil or melted butter, for greasing (if using)
- 9 oz/250 g cooked peeled shrimp
- 2 cups all-purpose flour
- 1 tbsp baking powder
- ⅛ tsp salt
- freshly ground black pepper
- 2 large eggs
- 1 cup buttermilk
- 6 tbsp sunflower oil or melted, cooled butter
- 3 tbsp chopped fresh parsley

Tuna & Olive Muffins

1. Preheat the oven to 400°F/200°C. Grease a 12-cup muffin pan or line with 12 muffin paper liners. Coarsely chop the olives, reserving 12 whole ones to garnish.

2. Sift together the flour, baking powder, salt, and pepper to taste into a large bowl. Stir in the chopped olives.

3. Lightly beat the eggs in a large pitcher or bowl, then beat in the buttermilk and oil. Make a well in the center of the dry ingredients, pour in the beaten liquid ingredients, and add the tuna. Stir gently until just combined; do not overmix.

4. Spoon the batter into the prepared muffin pan. Top each muffin with one of the reserved olives. Bake in the preheated oven for about 20 minutes, until well risen, golden brown, and firm to the touch.

5. Let the muffins cool in the pan for 5 minutes, then serve warm.

Makes 12

* oil or melted butter, for greasing (if using)
* ½ cup pitted black olives
* 2 cups all-purpose flour
* 1 tbsp baking powder
* ⅛ tsp salt
* freshly ground black pepper
* 2 large eggs
* 1 cup buttermilk
* 6 tbsp sunflower oil or melted, cooled butter
* 14 oz/400g canned tuna in olive oil, drained and flaked

Chicken & Corn Muffins

1. Preheat the oven to 400°F/200°C. Grease a 12-cup muffin pan or line with 12 muffin paper liners. Heat 1 tablespoon of the oil in a skillet. Add the onion and cook for 2 minutes. Add the chicken and cook for about 5 minutes, stirring occasionally, until tender. Remove from the heat and let cool.

2. Meanwhile, sift together the flour, baking powder, salt, and pepper to taste into a large bowl.

3. Lightly beat the eggs in a large pitcher or bowl, then beat in the buttermilk and remaining oil. Make a well in the center of the dry ingredients, pour in the beaten liquid ingredients, and add the chicken mixture and corn. Stir gently until just combined; do not overmix.

4. Spoon the batter into the prepared muffin pan. Bake in the preheated oven for about 20 minutes, until well risen, golden brown, and firm to the touch.

5. Let the muffins cool in the pan for 5 minutes, sprinkle with paprika, and serve warm.

Makes 12

* oil or melted butter, for greasing (if using)
* 7 tbsp sunflower oil
* 1 onion, finely chopped
* 1 skinless chicken breast, about 6 oz/175 g, finely chopped
* 2 cups all-purpose flour
* 1 tbsp baking powder
* ⅛ tsp salt
* freshly ground black pepper
* 2 large eggs
* 1 cup buttermilk
* ½ cup frozen corn kernels
* ground paprika, to garnish

Spicy Chorizo Muffins

1. Preheat the oven to 400°F/200°C. Grease a 12-cup muffin pan or line with 12 muffin paper liners. Sift together the flour, baking powder, salt, and paprika into a large bowl. Stir in the chorizo sausage and red bell pepper.

2. Lightly beat the eggs in a large pitcher or bowl, then beat in the buttermilk, oil, and garlic. Make a well in the center of the dry ingredients and pour in the beaten liquid ingredients. Stir gently until just combined; do not overmix.

3. Spoon the batter into the prepared muffin pan. Bake in the preheated oven for about 20 minutes, until well risen, golden brown, and firm to the touch.

4. Let the muffins cool in the pan for 5 minutes, sprinkle with paprika, and serve warm.

Makes 12

* oil or melted butter, for greasing (if using)
* 2 cups all-purpose flour
* 1 tbsp baking powder
* ⅛ tsp salt
* 1 tsp ground paprika, plus extra to garnish
* 3½ oz/100 g chorizo sausage, outer casing removed, finely chopped
* 1 small red bell pepper, cored, seeded, and finely chopped
* 2 large eggs
* 1 cup buttermilk
* 6 tbsp sunflower oil or melted, cooled butter
* 1 garlic clove, crushed

74

Crispy Bacon Muffins

① Preheat the oven to 400°F/200°C. Grease a 12-cup muffin pan or line with 12 muffin paper liners. Chop the bacon, reserving 3 strips to garnish. Cut each of the reserved bacon strips into four pieces.

② Heat 1 tablespoon of the oil in a skillet. Add the onion and cook for 2 minutes. Add the chopped bacon and cook for about 5 minutes, stirring occasionally, until crispy. Remove from the heat and let cool.

③ Meanwhile, sift together the flour, baking powder, salt, and pepper to taste into a large bowl.

④ Lightly beat the eggs in a large pitcher or bowl, then beat in the buttermilk and remaining oil. Make a well in the center of the dry ingredients, pour in the beaten liquid ingredients, and add the bacon mixture. Stir gently until just combined; do not overmix.

⑤ Spoon the batter into the prepared muffin pan. Place one of the reserved pieces of bacon on top of each muffin. Bake in the preheated oven for about 20 minutes, until well risen, golden brown, and firm to the touch.

⑥ Let the muffins cool in the pan for 5 minutes, then serve warm.

Makes 12

- oil or melted butter, for greasing (if using)
- 9 oz/250 g rindless, smoked lean bacon
- 7 tbsp sunflower oil
- 1 onion, finely chopped
- 2 cups all-purpose flour
- 1 tbsp baking powder
- ⅛ tsp salt
- freshly ground black pepper
- 2 large eggs
- 1 cup buttermilk

75

Pepperoni & Sun-Dried Tomato Muffins

1. Preheat the oven to 400°F/200°C. Grease a 12-cup muffin pan or line with 12 muffin paper liners. Sift together the flour, baking powder, salt, and pepper to taste into a large bowl. Stir in the oregano, sun-dried tomatoes, and pepperoni.

2. Lightly beat the eggs in a large pitcher or bowl, then beat in the buttermilk, 6 tablespoons of the reserved oil from the tomatoes, and the garlic. Make a well in the center of the dry ingredients and pour in the beaten liquid ingredients. Stir gently until just combined; do not overmix.

3. Spoon the batter into the prepared muffin pan. Bake in the preheated oven for about 20 minutes, until well risen, golden brown, and firm to the touch.

4. Let the muffins cool in the pan for 5 minutes, then serve warm.

Makes 12

* oil or melted butter, for greasing (if using)
* 2 cups all-purpose flour
* 1 tbsp baking powder
* ⅛ tsp salt
  freshly ground black pepper
  1 tsp dried oregano
  ½ cup sun-dried tomatoes in oil, drained (oil reserved) and finely chopped
  3½ oz/100 g pepperoni slices, finely chopped
* 2 large eggs
* 1 cup buttermilk
  1 garlic clove, crushed

Zucchini & Sesame Seed Muffins

1. Preheat the oven to 400°F/200°C. Grease a 12-cup muffin pan or line with 12 muffin paper liners. Grate the zucchini, squeezing out any excess moisture.

2. Sift together the flour, baking powder, salt, and pepper to taste into a large bowl. Stir in 4 teaspoons of the sesame seeds and the mixed herbs.

3. Lightly beat the eggs in a large pitcher or bowl, then beat in the buttermilk and oil. Make a well in the center of the dry ingredients, pour in the beaten liquid ingredients, and add the grated zucchini. Stir gently until just combined; do not overmix.

4. Spoon the batter into the prepared muffin pan. Scatter the remaining 2 teaspoons of sesame seeds over the tops of the muffins. Bake in the preheated oven for about 20 minutes, until well risen, golden brown, and firm to the touch.

5. Let the muffins cool in the pan for 5 minutes, then serve warm.

Makes 12

* oil or melted butter, for greasing (if using)
* 2 medium, firm zucchini, about 10½ oz/300 g
* 2 cups all-purpose flour
* 1 tbsp baking powder
* ⅛ tsp salt
* freshly ground black pepper
* 2 tbsp sesame seeds
* ½ tsp dried mixed herbs
* 2 large eggs
* 1 cup buttermilk
* 6 tbsp sunflower oil or melted, cooled butter

Spinach & Nutmeg Muffins

1. Preheat the oven to 400°F/200°C. Grease a 12-cup muffin pan or line with 12 muffin paper liners. Put the spinach in a strainer and drain well, squeezing out as much of the moisture as possible.

2. Heat 2 tablespoons of the oil in a skillet. Add the onion and cook for about 3 minutes, until beginning to soften. Add the garlic and cook for 1 minute. Add the spinach and cook for an additional 2 minutes, stirring all the time. Remove from the heat and let cool.

3. Meanwhile, sift together the flour, baking powder, nutmeg, salt, and pepper to taste into a large bowl.

4. Lightly beat the eggs in a large pitcher or bowl, then beat in the buttermilk and remaining oil. Make a well in the center of the dry ingredients, pour in the beaten liquid ingredients, and add the spinach mixture. Stir gently until just combined; do not overmix.

5. Spoon the batter into the prepared muffin pan. Scatter the pine nuts over the tops of the muffins. Bake in the preheated oven for about 20 minutes, until well risen, golden brown, and firm to the touch.

6. Let the muffins cool in the pan for 5 minutes, then serve warm.

Makes 12

- oil or melted butter, for greasing (if using)
- 9 oz/250 g frozen chopped spinach, thawed
- 8 tbsp sunflower oil
- 1 onion, finely chopped
- 1 garlic clove, finely chopped
- 2 cups all-purpose flour
- 1 tbsp baking powder
- ½ tsp freshly grated nutmeg
- ⅛ tsp salt
- freshly ground black pepper
- 2 large eggs
- 1 cup buttermilk
- ¼ cup pine nuts

Caramelized Onion Muffins

1. Preheat the oven to 400°F/200°C. Grease a 12-cup muffin pan or line with 12 muffin paper liners. Heat 2 tablespoons of the oil in a skillet. Add the onions and cook for about 3 minutes, until beginning to soften. Add the vinegar and sugar and cook, stirring occasionally, for an additional 10 minutes, until golden brown. Remove from the heat and let cool.

2. Meanwhile, sift together the flour, baking powder, salt, and pepper to taste into a large bowl.

3. Lightly beat the eggs in a large pitcher or bowl, then beat in the buttermilk and remaining oil. Make a well in the center of the dry ingredients, pour in the beaten liquid ingredients, and add the onion mixture, reserving 4 tablespoons for the topping. Stir gently until just combined; do not overmix.

4. Spoon the batter into the prepared muffin pan. Sprinkle the reserved onion mixture over the tops of the muffins. Bake in the preheated oven for about 20 minutes, until well risen, golden brown, and firm to the touch.

5. Let the muffins cool in the pan for 5 minutes, then serve warm.

Makes 12

- oil or melted butter, for greasing (if using)
- 7 tbsp sunflower oil
- 3 onions, finely chopped
- 1 tbsp red wine vinegar
- 2 tsp sugar
- 2 cups all-purpose flour
- 1 tbsp baking powder
- ⅛ tsp salt
- freshly ground black pepper
- 2 large eggs
- 1 cup buttermilk

Asparagus & Sour Cream Muffins

1. Preheat the oven to 400°F/200°C. Grease a 12-cup muffin pan or line with 12 muffin paper liners. Put 1 tablespoon of the oil in a roasting pan. Add the asparagus and turn in the oil. Roast in the oven for 10 minutes, until tender. When cool enough to handle, coarsely chop the asparagus.

2. Sift together the flour, baking powder, salt, and pepper to taste into a large bowl. Stir in the asparagus.

3. Lightly beat the eggs in a large pitcher or bowl, then beat in the sour cream and remaining oil. Make a well in the center of the dry ingredients and pour in the beaten liquid ingredients. Stir gently until just combined; do not overmix.

4. Spoon the batter into the prepared muffin pan. Scatter the cheddar cheese over the tops of the muffins. Bake in the preheated oven for about 20 minutes, until well risen, golden brown, and firm to the touch.

5. Let the muffins cool in the pan for 5 minutes, then serve warm.

Makes 12

* oil or melted butter, for greasing (if using)
* 7 tbsp sunflower oil
* 8 oz/225 g fresh asparagus
* 2 cups all-purpose flour
* 1 tbsp baking powder
* ⅛ tsp salt
* freshly ground black pepper
* 2 large eggs
* 1 cup sour cream
* ⅓ cup finely grated cheddar cheese

80

Tomato & Basil Muffins

1. Preheat the oven to 400°F/200°C. Grease a 12-cup muffin pan or line with 12 muffin paper liners. Sift together the flour, baking powder, salt, and pepper to taste into a large bowl. Stir in the sun-dried tomatoes.

2. Lightly beat the eggs in a large pitcher or bowl, then beat in the buttermilk, 6 tablespoons of the reserved oil from the tomatoes, the basil, and garlic. Make a well in the center of the dry ingredients and pour in the beaten liquid ingredients. Stir gently until just combined; do not overmix.

3. Spoon the batter into the prepared muffin pan. Scatter the Parmesan cheese over the tops of the muffins. Bake in the preheated oven for about 20 minutes, until well risen, golden brown, and firm to the touch.

4. Let the muffins cool in the pan for 5 minutes, then serve warm.

Makes 12

* oil or melted butter, for greasing (if using)
* 2 cups all-purpose flour
* 1 tbsp baking powder
* ⅛ tsp salt
  freshly ground black pepper
  scant ¾ cup sun-dried tomatoes in oil, drained (oil reserved) and finely chopped
* 2 large eggs
* 1 cup buttermilk
  4 tbsp chopped fresh basil leaves
  1 garlic clove, crushed
  4 tsp freshly grated Parmesan cheese

Italian Pesto Muffins

1. Preheat the oven to 400°F/200°C. Grease a 12-cup muffin pan or line with 12 muffin paper liners. Sift together the flour, baking powder, salt, and pepper to taste into a large bowl. Stir in the pine nuts.

2. Lightly beat the eggs in a large pitcher or bowl, then beat in the buttermilk, oil, and pesto. Make a well in the center of the dry ingredients and pour in the beaten liquid ingredients. Stir gently until just combined; do not overmix.

3. Spoon the batter into the prepared muffin pan. Scatter the Parmesan cheese over the tops of the muffins. Bake in the preheated oven for about 20 minutes, until well risen, golden brown, and firm to the touch.

4. Let the muffins cool in the pan for 5 minutes, then serve warm.

Makes 12

* oil or melted butter, for greasing (if using)
* 2 cups all-purpose flour
* 1 tbsp baking powder
* ⅛ tsp salt
  freshly ground black pepper
  heaping ¼ cup pine nuts
* 2 large eggs
  ⅔ cup buttermilk
* 6 tbsp sunflower oil or melted, cooled butter
  6 tbsp pesto
  4 tsp freshly grated Parmesan cheese

Carrot & Cilantro Muffins

1. Preheat the oven to 400°F/200°C. Grease a 12-cup muffin pan or line with 12 muffin paper liners. Sift together the flour, baking powder, salt, and pepper to taste into a large bowl. Stir in the grated carrots.

2. Lightly beat the eggs in a large pitcher or bowl, then beat in the buttermilk, oil, and chopped cilantro. Make a well in the center of the dry ingredients and pour in the beaten liquid ingredients. Stir gently until just combined; do not overmix.

3. Spoon the batter into the prepared muffin pan. Bake in the preheated oven for about 20 minutes, until well risen, golden brown, and firm to the touch.

4. Let the muffins cool in the pan for 5 minutes, then serve warm, garnished with sprigs of cilantro.

Makes 12

* oil or melted butter, for greasing (if using)
* 2 cups all-purpose flour
* 1 tbsp baking powder
* ⅛ tsp salt
  freshly ground black pepper
  1 cup grated carrots
* 2 large eggs
* 1 cup buttermilk
* 6 tbsp sunflower oil or melted, cooled butter
  3 tbsp chopped fresh cilantro, plus extra sprigs to garnish

Healthy

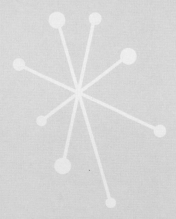

83

Whole Wheat Banana Muffins

1. Put the raisins in a bowl, add the orange juice, and let soak for 1 hour. Grease a 12-cup muffin pan or line with 12 muffin paper liners.

2. Preheat the oven to 400°F/200°C. Sift together both types of flour and the baking powder into a large bowl, adding any bran left in the sifter. Stir in the sugar.

3. Mash the bananas and put in a pitcher. Make up the puree to a scant 1 cup with milk.

4. Lightly beat the eggs in a large pitcher or bowl, then beat in the banana and milk mixture, oil, soaked raisins, and orange rind. Make a well in the center of the dry ingredients and pour in the beaten liquid ingredients. Stir gently until just combined; do not overmix.

5. Spoon the batter into the prepared muffin pan. Bake in the preheated oven for about 20 minutes, until well risen, golden brown, and firm to the touch.

6. Let the muffins cool in the pan for 5 minutes, then serve warm or transfer to a wire rack and let cool completely.

Makes 12

⅓ cup raisins

3 tbsp fresh orange juice

✳ oil or melted butter, for greasing (if using)

1 cup all-purpose flour

1 cup whole wheat flour

✳ 1 tbsp baking powder

✳ heaping ½ cup superfine sugar

2 bananas

about scant ½ cup skim milk

✳ 2 large eggs

✳ 6 tbsp sunflower oil

grated rind of 1 orange

84

Lemon Cornmeal Muffins

1. Preheat the oven to 400°F/200°C. Grease a 12-cup muffin pan or line with 12 muffin paper liners. Finely grate the rind from the lemons and squeeze the juice. Make up the juice to 1 cup with yogurt and add the lemon rind.

2. Sift in the flour, baking powder, and baking soda into a large bowl. Stir in the cornmeal and sugar.

3. Lightly beat the eggs in a large pitcher or bowl, then beat in the oil. Make a well in the center of the dry ingredients and pour in the beaten liquid ingredients. Stir gently until just combined; do not overmix.

4. Spoon the batter into the prepared muffin pan. Bake in the preheated oven for about 20 minutes, until well risen, golden brown, and firm to the touch.

5. Let the muffins cool in the pan for 5 minutes, then serve warm or transfer to a wire rack and let cool completely.

Makes 12

* oil or melted butter, for greasing (if using)
* 4 lemons
* about 3 tbsp low-fat plain yogurt
* 1¼ cups all-purpose flour
* 1 tbsp baking powder
* ½ tsp baking soda
* scant 2 cups yellow cornmeal
* heaping ½ cup superfine sugar
* 2 large eggs
* 6 tbsp sunflower oil

Low-Fat Muffins

1. Preheat the oven to 400°F/200°C. Grease a 12-cup muffin pan or line with 12 muffin paper liners. Sift together the flour, baking powder, and baking soda into a large bowl. Stir in the sugar.

2. Lightly beat the egg whites in a large pitcher or bowl, then beat in the yogurt, oil, and vanilla extract. Make a well in the center of the dry ingredients and pour in the beaten liquid ingredients. Stir gently until just combined; do not overmix

3. Spoon the batter into the prepared muffin pan. Bake in the preheated oven for about 20 minutes, until well risen, golden brown, and firm to the touch.

4. Let the muffins cool in the pan for 5 minutes, then serve warm.

Makes 12

* oil or melted butter, for greasing (if using)
* 2 cups all-purpose flour
* 1 tbsp baking powder
* ½ tsp baking soda
* heaping ½ cup superfine sugar
* 2 extra large egg whites
* 1 cup low-fat plain yogurt
* 3 tbsp sunflower oil
* 1 tsp vanilla extract

Shredded Vegetable Muffins

1. Preheat the oven to 400°F/200°C. Grease a 12-cup muffin pan or line with 12 muffin paper liners. Grate the zucchini, squeezing out any excess moisture. Put in a bowl and grate in the carrots.

2. Sift together both types of flour and the baking powder into a large bowl, adding any bran left in the sifter. Stir in the sugar and golden raisins.

3. Lightly beat the eggs in a large pitcher or bowl, then beat in the buttermilk and oil. Make a well in the center of the dry ingredients, pour in the beaten liquid ingredients, and add the grated vegetables. Stir gently until just combined; do not overmix.

4. Spoon the batter into the prepared muffin pan. Bake in the preheated oven for about 20 minutes, until well risen, golden brown, and firm to the touch.

5. Let the muffins cool in the pan for 5 minutes, then serve warm or transfer to a wire rack and let cool completely.

Makes 12

* oil or melted butter, for greasing (if using)
  4½ oz/125 g firm zucchini
  4½ oz/125 g carrots
  1 cup whole wheat flour
  1 cup all-purpose flour
* 1 tbsp baking powder
* heaping ½ cup superfine sugar
  heaping ¼ cup golden raisins
* 2 large eggs
* 1 cup buttermilk
* 6 tbsp sunflower oil

87

Oat & Cranberry Muffins

1. Preheat the oven to 400°F/200°C. Grease a 12-cup muffin pan or line with 12 muffin paper liners. Sift together the flour and baking powder into a large bowl. Stir in the sugar, oats, and cranberries.

2. Lightly beat the eggs in a large pitcher or bowl, then beat in the buttermilk, oil, and vanilla extract. Make a well in the center of the dry ingredients and pour in the beaten liquid ingredients. Stir gently until just combined; do not overmix.

3. Spoon the batter into the prepared muffin pan. Bake in the preheated oven for about 20 minutes, until well risen, golden brown, and firm to the touch.

4. Let the muffins cool in the pan for 5 minutes, then serve warm or transfer to a wire rack and let cool completely.

Makes 12

- oil or melted butter, for greasing (if using)
- 1 cup all-purpose flour
- 1 tbsp baking powder
- heaping ½ cup firmly packed dark brown sugar
- scant 2 cups rolled oats
- ¾ cup dried cranberries
- 2 large eggs
- 1 cup buttermilk
- 6 tbsp sunflower oil
- 1 tsp vanilla extract

Muesli Muffins

1. Preheat the oven to 400°F/200°C. Grease a 12-cup muffin pan or line with 12 muffin paper liners. Sift together the flour and baking powder into a large bowl. Stir in the muesli and sugar.

2. Lightly beat the eggs in a large pitcher or bowl, then beat in the buttermilk and oil. Make a well in the center of the dry ingredients and pour in the beaten liquid ingredients. Stir gently until just combined; do not overmix.

3. Spoon the batter into the prepared muffin pan. Bake in the preheated oven for about 20 minutes, until well risen, golden brown, and firm to the touch.

4. Let the muffins cool in the pan for 5 minutes, then serve warm or transfer to a wire rack and let cool completely.

Makes 12

* oil or melted butter, for greasing (if using)
  1 cup all-purpose flour
* 1 tbsp baking powder
  scant 2 cups unsweetened muesli
* heaping ½ cup firmly packed light brown sugar
* 2 large eggs
* 1 cup buttermilk
* 6 tbsp sunflower oil

Glazed Honey Muffins

1. Preheat the oven to 400°F/200°C. Grease a 12-cup muffin pan or line with 12 muffin paper liners. Sift together both types of flour, the baking powder, baking soda, and apple pie spice into a large bowl, adding any bran left in the sifter. Stir in the sugar and golden raisins.

2. Lightly beat the eggs in a large pitcher or bowl, then beat in the yogurt, oil, and 4 tablespoons of the honey. Make a well in the center of the dry ingredients and pour in the beaten liquid ingredients. Stir gently until just combined; do not overmix.

3. Spoon the batter into the prepared muffin pan. Bake in the preheated oven for about 20 minutes, until well risen, golden brown, and firm to the touch.

4. Let the muffins cool in the pan for 5 minutes, then drizzle about 1 teaspoon of the remaining honey on top of each muffin. Serve warm or transfer to a wire rack and let cool completely.

Makes 12

* oil or melted butter, for greasing (if using)
* 1 cup whole wheat flour
* 1 cup all-purpose flour
* 1 tbsp baking powder
* ½ tsp baking soda
* ½ tsp apple pie spice
* 4 tbsp light brown sugar
* heaping ½ cup golden raisins
* 2 large eggs
* scant 1 cup low-fat plain yogurt
* 6 tbsp sunflower oil
* 8 tbsp clear honey

90

Ginger Wheat Germ Muffins

1. Preheat the oven to 400°F/200°C. Grease a 12-cup muffin pan or line with 12 muffin paper liners. Sift together the flour, baking powder, and ground ginger into a large bowl. Stir in the sugar, wheat germ, and chopped ginger.

2. Lightly beat the eggs in a large pitcher or bowl, then beat in the milk and oil. Make a well in the center of the dry ingredients and pour in the beaten liquid ingredients. Stir gently until just combined; do not overmix.

3. Spoon the batter into the prepared muffin pan. Bake in the preheated oven for about 20 minutes, until well risen, golden brown, and firm to the touch.

4. Let the muffins cool in the pan for 5 minutes, then serve warm or transfer to a wire rack and let cool completely.

Makes 12

* oil or melted butter, for greasing (if using)
  1 cup all-purpose flour
* 1 tbsp baking powder
  4 tsp ground ginger
* heaping ½ cup firmly packed dark brown sugar
  scant 1½ cups wheat germ
  3 pieces preserved ginger in syrup, finely chopped
* 2 large eggs
* 1 cup skim milk
* 6 tbsp sunflower oil

Fresh Orange Muffins

1. Preheat the oven to 400°F/200°C. Grease a 12-cup muffin pan or line with 12 muffin paper liners. Finely grate the rind from 2 of the oranges and set aside. Using a serrated knife, remove the peel from all of the oranges, discarding the white pith. Cut the flesh into segments, reserving 6 segments. Cut the reserved segments in half and set aside. Coarsely chop the remaining orange segments.

2. Sift together both types of flour and the baking powder into a large bowl, adding any bran left in the sifter. Stir in the sugar.

3. Lightly beat the eggs in a large pitcher or bowl, then beat in the orange juice, oil, and reserved orange rind. Make a well in the center of the dry ingredients, pour in the beaten liquid ingredients, and add the chopped oranges. Stir gently until just combined; do not overmix.

4. Spoon the batter into the prepared muffin pan. Place the reserved halved orange segments on the tops of the muffins. Bake in the preheated oven for about 20 minutes, until well risen, golden brown, and firm to the touch.

5. Let the muffins cool in the pan for 5 minutes, then serve warm or transfer to a wire rack and let cool completely.

Makes 12

* oil or melted butter, for greasing (if using)
5 oranges
1 cup whole wheat flour
1 cup all-purpose flour
* 1 tbsp baking powder
* heaping ½ cup superfine sugar
* 2 large eggs
* 1 cup fresh orange juice
* 6 tbsp sunflower oil

Raisin Bran Muffins

1. Preheat the oven to 400°F/200°C. Grease a 12-cup muffin pan or line with 12 muffin paper liners. Sift together the flour and baking powder into a large bowl. Stir in the wheat bran, sugar, and raisins.

2. Lightly beat the eggs in a large pitcher or bowl, then beat in the milk, oil, and vanilla extract. Make a well in the center of the dry ingredients and pour in the beaten liquid ingredients. Stir gently until just combined; do not overmix.

3. Spoon the batter into the prepared muffin pan. Bake in the preheated oven for about 20 minutes, until well risen, golden brown, and firm to the touch.

4. Let the muffins cool in the pan for 5 minutes, then serve warm or transfer to a wire rack and let cool completely.

Makes 12

* oil or melted butter, for greasing (if using)
* 1 cup all-purpose flour
* 1 tbsp baking powder
* 2¼ cups wheat bran
* heaping ½ cup superfine sugar
* 1 cup raisins
* 2 large eggs
* 1 cup skim milk
* 6 tbsp sunflower oil
* 1 tsp vanilla extract

93

Spicy Apple & Oat Muffins

1. Preheat the oven to 400°F/200°C. Grease a 12-cup muffin pan or line with 12 muffin paper liners. Sift together the flour, baking powder, and apple pie spice into a large bowl. Stir in the sugar and scant 1 cup of the oats.

2. Finely chop the unpeeled apples, discarding the cores. Add to the flour mixture and stir together.

3. Lightly beat the eggs in a large pitcher or bowl, then beat in the milk, apple juice, and oil. Make a well in the center of the dry ingredients and pour in the beaten liquid ingredients. Stir gently until just combined; do not overmix.

4. Spoon the batter into the prepared muffin pan. Sprinkle the tops of the muffins with the remaining oats. Bake in the preheated oven for about 20 minutes, until well risen, golden brown, and firm to the touch.

5. Let the muffins cool in the pan for 5 minutes, then serve warm or transfer to a wire rack and let cool completely.

Makes 12

* oil or melted butter, for greasing (if using)
  1 cup all-purpose flour
* 1 tbsp baking powder
  1 tsp apple pie spice
* heaping ½ cup firmly packed light brown sugar
  heaped 2 cups rolled oats
  9 oz/250 g apples
* 2 large eggs
  ½ cup skimmed milk
  ½ cup fresh apple juice
* 6 tbsp sunflower oil

Sunflower Seed Muffins

1. Preheat the oven to 400°F/200°C. Grease a 12-cup muffin pan or line with 12 muffin paper liners. Sift together the flour and baking powder into a large bowl. Stir in the sugar, oats, golden raisins, and heaping ½ cup of the sunflower seeds.

2. Lightly beat the eggs in a large pitcher or bowl, then beat in the milk, oil, and vanilla extract. Make a well in the center of the dry ingredients and pour in the beaten liquid ingredients. Stir gently until just combined; do not overmix.

3. Spoon the batter into the prepared muffin pan. Sprinkle the remaining sunflower seeds over the tops of the muffins. Bake in the preheated oven for about 20 minutes, until well risen, golden brown, and firm to the touch.

4. Let the muffins cool in the pan for 5 minutes, then serve warm or transfer to a wire rack and let cool completely.

Makes 12

* oil or melted butter, for greasing (if using)
* 1 cup all-purpose flour
* 1 tbsp baking powder
* heaping ½ cup firmly packed light brown sugar
* scant 2 cups rolled oats
* heaping ½ cup golden raisins
* ¾ cup sunflower seeds
* 2 large eggs
* 1 cup skim milk
* 6 tbsp sunflower oil
* 1 tsp vanilla extract

Three-Grain Muffins

1. Preheat the oven to 400°F/200°C. Grease a 12-cup muffin pan or line with 12 muffin paper liners. Sift together both types of flour and the baking powder into a large bowl, adding any bran left in the sifter. Stir in the sugar, cornmeal, and oats.

2. Lightly beat the eggs in a large pitcher or bowl, then beat in the buttermilk, oil, and vanilla extract. Make a well in the center of the dry ingredients and pour in the beaten liquid ingredients. Stir gently until just combined; do not overmix.

3. Spoon the batter into the prepared muffin pan. Bake in the preheated oven for about 20 minutes, until well risen, golden brown, and firm to the touch.

4. Let the muffins cool in the pan for 5 minutes, then serve warm or transfer to a wire rack and let cool completely.

Makes 12

* oil or melted butter, for greasing (if using)
  ½ cup whole wheat flour
  ½ cup all-purpose flour
* 1 tbsp baking powder
* heaping ½ cup firmly packed dark brown sugar
  heaping ¼ cup yellow cornmeal
  scant 1 cup rolled oats
* 2 large eggs
* 1 cup buttermilk
* 6 tbsp sunflower oil
* 1 tsp vanilla extract

96

Yogurt & Spice Muffins

1. Preheat the oven to 400°F/200°C. Grease a 12-cup muffin pan or line with 12 muffin paper liners. Sift together both types of flour, the baking powder, baking soda, and apple pie spice into a large bowl, adding any bran left in the sifter. Stir in the sugar and mixed dried fruit.

2. Lightly beat the eggs in a large pitcher or bowl, then beat in the yogurt and oil. Make a well in the center of the dry ingredients and pour in the beaten liquid ingredients. Stir gently until just combined; do not overmix.

3. Spoon the batter into the prepared muffin pan. Bake in the preheated oven for about 20 minutes, until well risen, golden brown, and firm to the touch.

4. Let the muffins cool in the pan for 5 minutes, then serve warm or transfer to a wire rack and let cool completely.

Makes 12

- ✳ oil or melted butter, for greasing (if using)
- 1 cup whole wheat flour
- 1 cup all-purpose flour
- ✳ 1 tbsp baking powder
- ✳ ½ tsp baking soda
- 4 tsp apple pie spice
- ✳ heaping ½ cup superfine sugar
- heaping ½ cup mixed dried fruit
- ✳ 2 large eggs
- ✳ 1 cup low-fat plain yogurt
- ✳ 6 tbsp sunflower oil

Wheat Germ, Banana &
Pumpkin Seed Muffins

1. Preheat the oven to 400°F/200°C. Grease a 12-cup muffin pan or line with 12 muffin paper liners. Sift together the flour and baking powder into a large bowl. Stir in the sugar, wheat germ, and heaping ¼ cup of the pumpkin seeds.

2. Mash the bananas and put in a pitcher. Make up the puree to 1 cup with milk.

3. Lightly beat the eggs in a large pitcher or bowl, then beat in the banana and milk mixture and the oil. Make a well in the center of the dry ingredients and pour in the beaten liquid ingredients. Stir gently until just combined; do not overmix.

4. Spoon the batter into the prepared muffin pan. Sprinkle the remaining pumpkin seeds over the tops of the muffins. Bake in the preheated oven for about 20 minutes, until well risen, golden brown, and firm to the touch.

5. Let the muffins cool in the pan for 5 minutes, then serve warm or transfer to a wire rack and let cool completely.

Makes 12

* oil or melted butter, for greasing (if using)
1 cup all-purpose flour
* 1 tbsp baking powder
* heaping ½ cup superfine sugar
scant 2 cups wheat germ
½ cup pumpkin seeds
2 bananas
about ⅔ cup skim milk
* 2 large eggs
* 6 tbsp sunflower oil

Healthy Oat & Prune Muffins

1. Preheat the oven to 400°F/200°C. Grease a 12-cup muffin pan or line with 12 muffin paper liners. Sift together the flour and baking powder into a large bowl. Stir in the sugar, oats, and prunes.

2. Lightly beat the eggs in a large pitcher or bowl, then beat in the buttermilk, oil, and vanilla extract. Make a well in the center of the dry ingredients and pour in the beaten liquid ingredients. Stir gently until just combined; do not overmix.

3. Spoon the batter into the prepared muffin pan. Bake in the preheated oven for about 20 minutes, until well risen, golden brown, and firm to the touch.

4. Let the muffins cool in the pan for 5 minutes, then serve warm or transfer to a wire rack and let cool completely.

Makes 12

* oil or melted butter, for greasing (if using)
* 1 cup all-purpose flour
* 1 tbsp baking powder
* heaping ½ cup firmly packed light brown sugar
* scant 2 cups rolled oats
* heaping ¾ cup pitted prunes, chopped
* 2 large eggs
* 1 cup buttermilk
* 6 tbsp sunflower oil
* 1 tsp vanilla extract

99

High-Fiber Muffins

1. Preheat the oven to 400°F/200°C. Grease a 12-cup muffin pan or line with 12 muffin paper liners. Put the cereal and milk in a bowl and let soak for about 5 minutes, until the cereal has softened.

2. Meanwhile, sift together the flour, baking powder, cinnamon, and nutmeg into a large bowl. Stir in the sugar and raisins.

3. Lightly beat the eggs in a large pitcher or bowl, then beat in the oil. Make a well in the center of the dry ingredients, pour in the beaten liquid ingredients, and add the cereal mixture. Stir gently until just combined; do not overmix.

4. Spoon the batter into the prepared muffin pan. Bake in the preheated oven for about 20 minutes, until well risen, golden brown, and firm to the touch.

5. Let the muffins cool in the pan for 5 minutes, then serve warm or transfer to a wire rack and let cool completely.

Makes 12

* oil or melted butter, for greasing (if using)
* 2 cups high-fiber bran cereal
* 1 cup skim milk
* 1 cup all-purpose flour
* 1 tbsp baking powder
* 1 tsp ground cinnamon
* ½ tsp freshly grated nutmeg
* heaping ½ cup superfine sugar
* scant ¾ cup raisins
* 2 large eggs
* 6 tbsp sunflower oil

100

Homemade Granola Muffins

1. To make the granola, put the oats in a large, dry skillet and toast over low heat for 1 minute. Add the almonds, sunflower seeds, and raisins and cook for an additional 6–8 minutes, until lightly browned. Add the sugar and stir quickly for 1 minute, until it melts. Remove from the heat and stir until well mixed.

2. Preheat the oven to 400°F/200°C. Grease a 12-cup muffin pan or line with 12 muffin paper liners. Sift together both types of flour and the baking powder into a large bowl, adding any bran left in the sifter. Stir in the sugar and the granola.

3. Lightly beat the eggs in a large pitcher or bowl, then beat in the milk and oil. Make a well in the center of the dry ingredients and pour in the beaten liquid ingredients. Stir gently until just combined; do not overmix.

4. Spoon the batter into the prepared muffin pan. Bake in the preheated oven for about 20 minutes, until well risen, golden brown, and firm to the touch.

5. Let the muffins cool in the pan for 5 minutes, then serve warm or transfer to a wire rack and let cool completely.

Makes 12

- oil or melted butter, for greasing (if using)
- 1 cup whole wheat flour
- 1 cup all-purpose flour
- 1 tbsp baking powder
- heaping ⅓ cup firmly packed light brown sugar
- 2 large eggs
- 1 cup skim milk
- 6 tbsp sunflower oil

For the granola
- scant 1 cup rolled oats
- 2 tbsp blanched almonds, chopped
- ¼ cup sunflower seeds
- scant ¼ cup raisins
- 2 tbsp light brown sugar